NORTH AMERICAN INDIANS

NORTH AMERICAN
INDIANS

Ottenheimer
PUBLISHERS, INC

This 1994 edition published by
Ottenheimer Publishers, Inc.
IN-002B

ISBN 0-8241-0019-0

Printed in China

Page 1: Zuñi Indian women, dressed in their ceremonial best and balancing elaborately decorated pots on their heads, attend the Inter-Tribal Indian Ceremonial that is held at Gallup, New Mexico every year.

Title page: A Charles Bird King portrait, painted in 1821, of a Pawnee delegation to Washington, the nation's capital.

Below: Life on the Plains rotated around the buffalo. In this 1895 photograph of a Cheyenne campsite, buffalo meat dries on racks alongside cleaned and sausage-stuffed entrails. The teepee, with the bottom raised for ventilation, is made of sewn-together buffalo hides.

Picture credits

American Graphic Systems Archives 7, 8, 9, 14, 15, 16, 17, 68, 69
Amon Carter Museum 2-3, 86-87, 90-91, 106-07, 142-43
Arizona Department of Tourism 182, 185 (top)
Coni Beeson 158, 159 (both), 166 (all 3), 167
Leslie Gray 60-61
Library of Congress 38-39
Lowie Museum of Anthropology, University of California, Berkeley 19, 20, 22 (both), 23, 25, 27, 29 (both), 30-31, 33, 58, 75, 99 (top), 140, 141, 144, 147 (top 2), 148, 149, 152 (both), 154, 155, 156 (lower right), 157, 160, 162 (bottom), 163 (bottom), 164 (both), 165 (top), 168 (all 3), 169 (both), 172, 177 (bottom), 180 (top), 181 (both), 185 (bottom right), 186, 187 (both)
Reverend M J McPike 126-27, 130 (top 2), 131
National Gallery of Art 43, 66-67
New Mexico State Economic Development/Tourism Department 1, 177 (top), 185 (bottom left), 188-89
North Carolina Travel and Tourism Office 81
Oklahoma Department of Tourism 81, 120
C M Russell Museum 115
Smithsonian Institution, National Anthropological Archives 4-5, 18-19, 20-21, 24-25, 27, 28 (both), 34-35, 34, 36, 36-37, 40, 49, 51, 53, 54-55, 56, 57, 64-65, 65, 72 (top), 73, 74, 76-77 (all 3), 78 (both), 79, 80 (both), 85, 88, 92-93 (both), 96, 99 (bottom 2), 100, 101, 104, 105, 108 (both), 109, 110 (all 3), 113 (both), 114, 116, 116-17, 124-25 (both), 128 (both), 129 (both), 130-31, 132, 133 (both), 134, 135, 136-37, 138-39, 145, 147 (bottom), 150-51, 152-53, 156 (top and lower left), 161, 165 (bottom 2), 172-73, 173, 176, 180 (bottom), 184 (both), 192
Smithsonian Institution, National Collection of Fine Arts 70, 82-83 (both), 90, 94-95, 98, 102-03
South Dakota Division of Tourism 89 (both), 121
South Dakota State Historical Society 97, 112, 117
Sutro Library 39, 40-41, 42 (both), 44 (both), 45 (both), 46 (both), 47, 48, 50, 52, 71, 72 (bottom)
US National Park Service 31
Bill Yenne 11, 118-19, 146, 162 (top), 163 (top), 174-75, 178, 179, 182-3, 183
Doris Yenne 32, 84

The authors would like to thank Rod Baird for his assistance in the picture research and pasteup; and Coni Beeson, Leslie Gray, Joan Holstein of the Arizona Department of Tourism and Gene Prince of the Lowie Museum of Anthropology, University of California at Berkeley for their kind assistance.

CONTENTS

The Arctic
The Subarctic
The Northwest Coast
The Great Basin
The Plains
California
The Southwest
The Northeast
The Southeast
Mesoamerica

Introduction

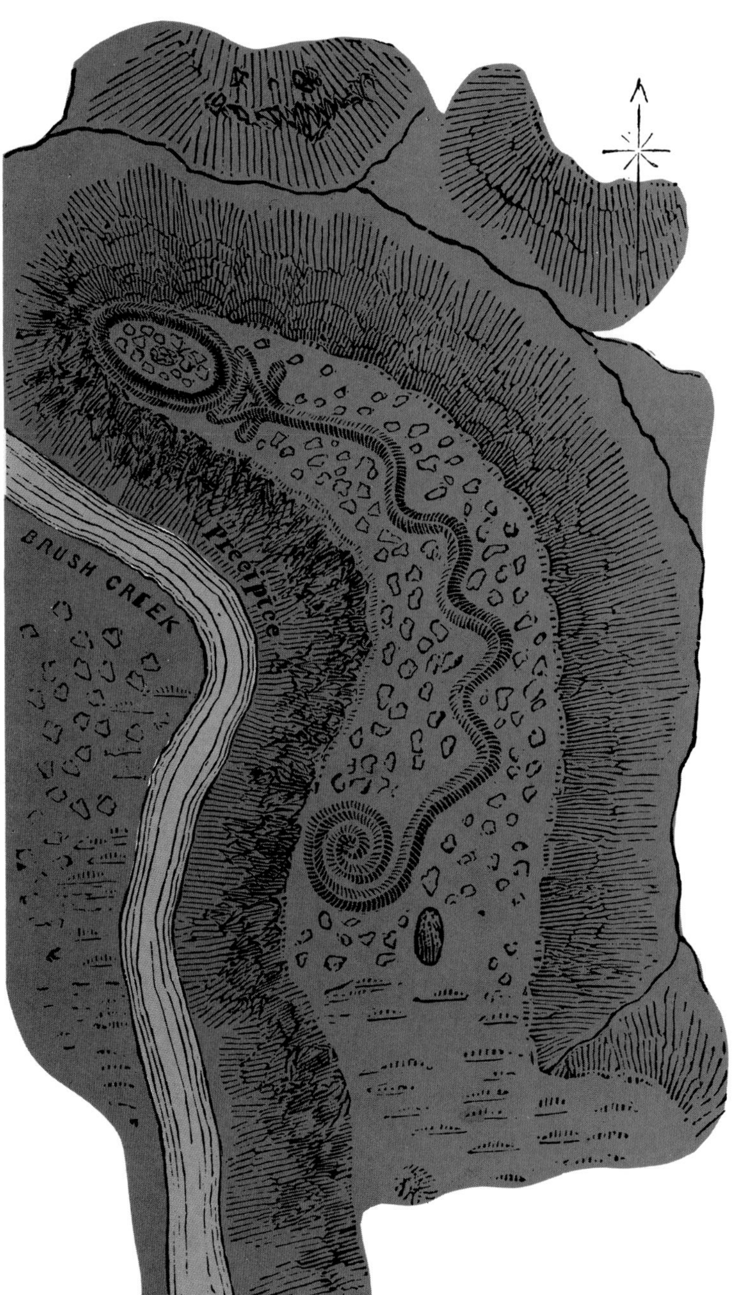

The history of North American peoples extends back into the dark recesses of the Ice Age, to about 50 millennia ago when vast glaciers covered most of Canada and Alaska, when the North American continent was void of any form of early modern man. As the massive ice layer crawled imperceptibly forward, soaking up the oceans and raising the seafloor, it created a bridge between Siberia and Alaska called the Bering Land Bridge. This slender passage was the gateway into North America for *Homo sapiens* from the tundras of Asia, Tibet and Indonesia who trudged their way westward in search of food.

The first migration was well underway by 10,000 BC according to archeologists, and possibly as early as 40,000 BC. The ingress ceased between 9000 and 8000 BC when the glacial retreat submerged the land bridge. East of the bridge across Alaskan territory the conditions were formidable at best, eased occasionally by warm periods, but small bands of individuals slowly penetrated the narrow access into Canada, trekking down the MacKenzie River into the Yukon Valley and onto the plains, east of the Rockies. By about 6000 BC the immigrants had infiltrated and occupied all parts of North and South America.

The story of the native North American is based on artifacts that have been discovered over the years. A chronology and rough timetable have been pieced together by archeologists and updated as new evidence arises. The archeological evidence shows that early Indian cultures were developing by 10,000 BC. As these hardy people progressed southward they discovered a land abounding in natural resources and swarming with the enormous ancestors of modern-day animals. These large bison, mammoths

Left: The Great Serpent Mound, near Cincinnati, Ohio, was the product of an advanced culture of Indians that developed around 1000 BC in the Ohio Valley. These ancient Indians were preoccupied with death and built these engineering wonders out of earth in a variety of animal or geometrical shapes, many with burial chambers concealed underneath. The Great Serpent mound is about 20 feet wide and over 1200 feet long. The burial chamber associated with it was built several hundred feet away and housed numerous bodies and cremated remains as well as a host of artifacts that were to accompany the dead to the Other World. This site, along with thousands of other mounds still in existence in the area, is a popular site for tourists.

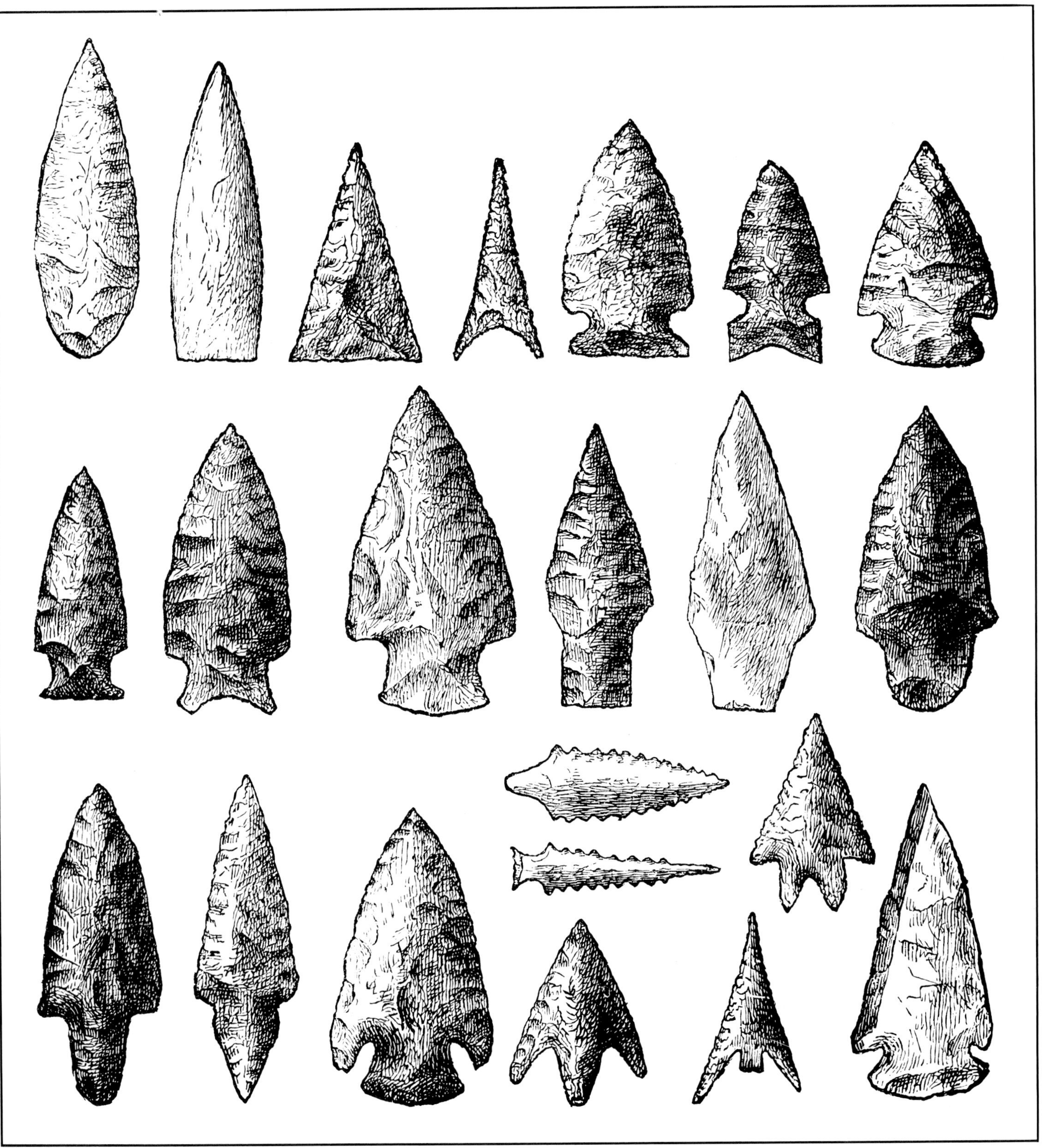

and mastadons the size of elephants, giant sloths, beavers and camels were their sole source of food. The following two thousand years or so are known as the Paleo-Indian period, the dawn of the Indian. Indians were big-game hunters in the Great Plains and in the Northeast. Evidence of large arrowhead-type weapons indicate that they were accomplished at that task. They were also wanderers. There are no indications that these people settled, built homes or stored food. They probably traveled in small bands and perhaps had to organize themselves to some degree in order to manage with such large prey.

The Ice Age gradually drew to a close and the glaciers retreated, causing profound changes in climate. Once wet and cold, it became drier and warmer, leaving desert in the

Left: These clay vessels retrieved from mounds of the Mississippi Valley were probably used for domestic purposes and are indicative of a highly developed culture and well-organized daily life. The mound builders of the Ohio Valley were replaced by a similar culture that developed 700 years later in the Mississippi Valley. This culture spread to cover the entire Mississippi Valley and it prospered for over 1000 years. The Mississippi Indians also built burial mounds, but they were much larger than the earlier Ohio structures and were built in layers. These underground tombs preserved the artistic accomplishments of this advanced early culture, evidence of the superb craftsmanship these Indians possessed.

Above: Early stone implements were fashioned by pounding them into the desired shape. These later arrowheads were made by a process of chipping the stone into the shape and size required. The slender (horizontal) arrowheads were probably used for carving or for leatherwork. The large arrowheads were probably attached to a shaft and used for hunting large game, while the smaller ones were reserved for small animals.

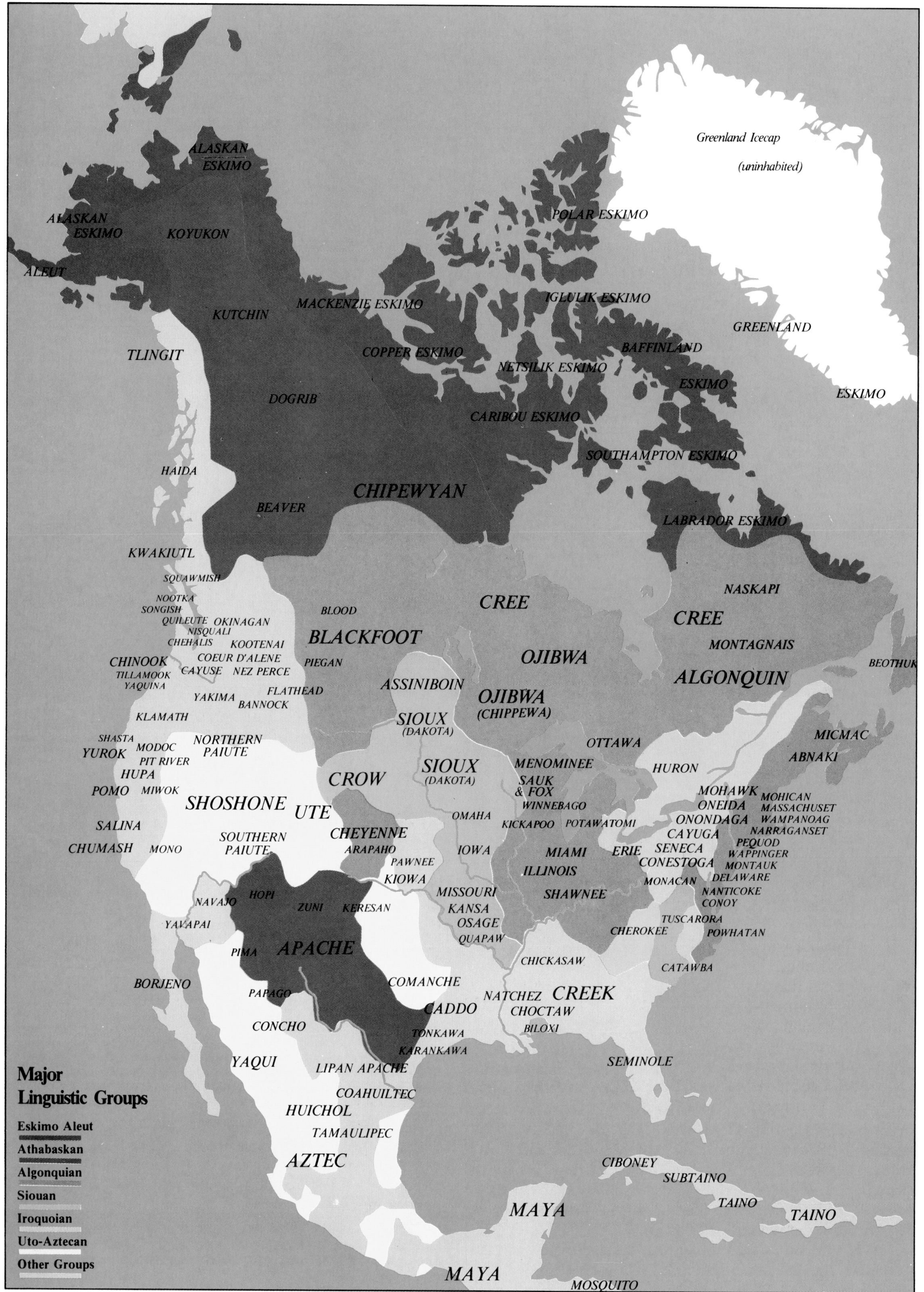
Greenland Icecap
(uninhabited)
ALASKAN ESKIMO
ALASKAN ESKIMO
KOYUKON
ALEUT
POLAR ESKIMO
KUTCHIN
MACKENZIE ESKIMO
IGLULIK ESKIMO
GREENLAND
TLINGIT
COPPER ESKIMO
NETSILIK ESKIMO
BAFFINLAND ESKIMO
ESKIMO
DOGRIB
CARIBOU ESKIMO
SOUTHAMPTON ESKIMO
HAIDA
CHIPEWYAN
BEAVER
LABRADOR ESKIMO
KWAKIUTL
SQUAWMISH
NOOTKA
SONGISH
QUILEUTE
NISQUALI
CHEHALIS
OKINAGAN
KOOTENAI
COEUR D'ALENE
NEZ PERCE
CAYUSE
CHINOOK
TILLAMOOK
YAQUINA
BLOOD
BLACKFOOT
PIEGAN
CREE
NASKAPI
CREE
MONTAGNAIS
OJIBWA
ALGONQUIN
BEOTHUK
ASSINIBOIN
OJIBWA
(CHIPPEWA)
FLATHEAD
YAKIMA
BANNOCK
KLAMATH
SIOUX
(DAKOTA)
SHASTA
MODOC
NORTHERN PAIUTE
YUROK
PIT RIVER
HUPA
POMO
MIWOK
SHOSHONE
UTE
CROW
SIOUX
(DAKOTA)
OTTAWA
MENOMINEE
SAUK & FOX
WINNEBAGO
HURON
MICMAC
ABNAKI
MOHAWK
ONEIDA
ONONDAGA
CAYUGA
SENECA
CONESTOGA
MOHICAN
MASSACHUSET
WAMPANOAG
NARRAGANSET
PEQUOD
WAPPINGER
MONTAUK
DELAWARE
NANTICOKE
CONOY
SALINA
CHUMASH
MONO
SOUTHERN PAIUTE
CHEYENNE
ARAPAHO
PAWNEE
KIOWA
OMAHA
IOWA
KICKAPOO
POTAWATOMI
MIAMI
ILLINOIS
ERIE
MONACAN
SHAWNEE
NAVAJO
HOPI
ZUNI
KERESAN
MISSOURI
KANSA
OSAGE
QUAPAW
YAVAPAI
TUSCARORA
CHEROKEE
POWHATAN
PIMA
APACHE
CHICKASAW
CATAWBA
BORJENO
COMANCHE
PAPAGO
NATCHEZ
CREEK
CHOCTAW
CADDO
BILOXI
CONCHO
TONKAWA
KARANKAWA
YAQUI
SEMINOLE
LIPAN APACHE
COAHUILTEC
HUICHOL
TAMAULIPEC
AZTEC
CIBONEY
SUBTAINO
TAINO
TAINO
MAYA
MAYA
MOSQUITO
Major Linguistic Groups
Eskimo Aleut
Athabaskan
Algonquian
Siouan
Iroquoian
Uto-Aztecan
Other Groups

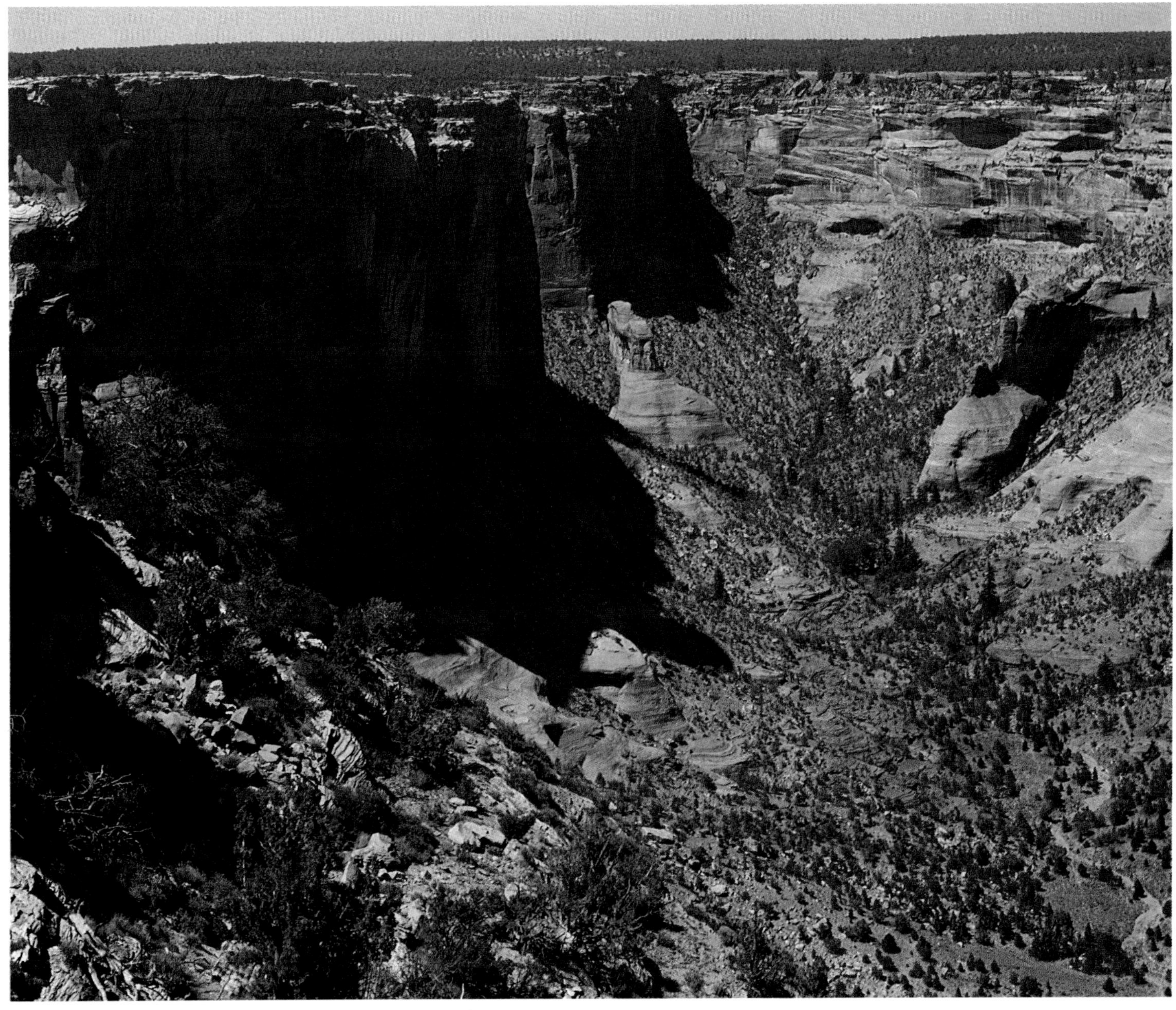

Above: The Anasazi people lived in caves and cliff shelters in the area where present-day states of New Mexico, Colorado, Utah and Arizona meet. They developed one of the most complex cultures to inhabit the southwestern part of North America.

Southwest, grassy plains and dense woodlands. The change in climate also affected animal life. About one half of the ancient species died out in this period, and the giant animals were replaced by smaller ones. As Indians reduced animal numbers in one area, they moved on to the next. They also learned to forage for vegetable matter. The Archaic Period, from about 8000 to 1000 BC, was one of mixed subsistence. Lifestyles became more stable. There are some signs that Indians were beginning to settle in the Northeast, to domesticate some livestock and to formulate complicated religious ideas.

Indians advanced more quickly in certain parts of the continent and developed skills according to their geographical location. As early as 5000 or 4000 BC Indians in the Great Lakes region were skilled at metalwork, the first metalworkers in North America. Various cultures of mound builders in the central valleys constructed enormous burial mounds, some in geometrical shapes, and left remnants of an abundance of wonderful art, but they were not agriculturalists. Ohio Valley Indians were competent traders, and by 1000 BC Indians in the east had begun farming.

The Archaic culture of the desert people in the Southwest reached Mexico around 7000 BC. By 4000 BC the ancient nomadic foragers were growing a crude form of corn and later a variety of vegetables. They were the first farmers of Middle and North America. By 2000 BC the cultures of Mesoamerica, which includes the area covering present-day Mexico, Honduras and Guatemala, had become fully agricultural. Indians settled in permament villages and life was transformed as in the north. In this region, however, sophisticated and large societies evolved systems of governments, complex religious ideas, arts and crafts, commerce and an architecture of an advanced quality unrivaled in North America.

The first civilization to develop in Mesoamerica, the Olmec, grew in southern Mexico between 1500 BC and 300 AD. It was a society run by priests and supported by the peasants who farmed the land. These early people left behind a massive stone pyramid, several immense carved stone heads, ceramics and intricate carvings as well as a calendar. Olmec culture spread to other parts of Mexico, but this center suddenly and mysteriously died out. An offshoot and more advanced Olmec tradition was carried on

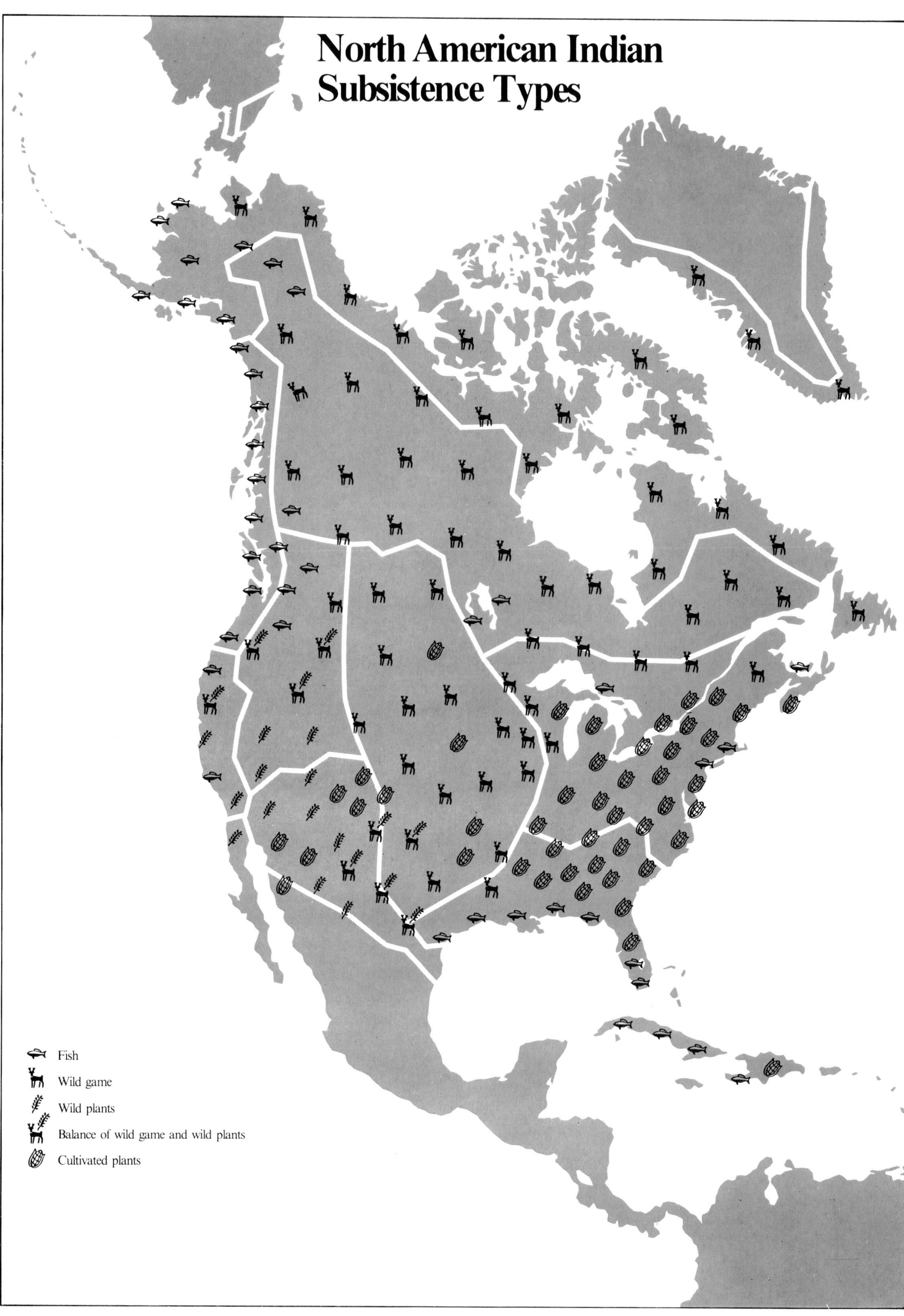
North American Indian
Subsistence Types
Fish
Wild game
Wild plants
Balance of wild game and wild plants
Cultivated plants

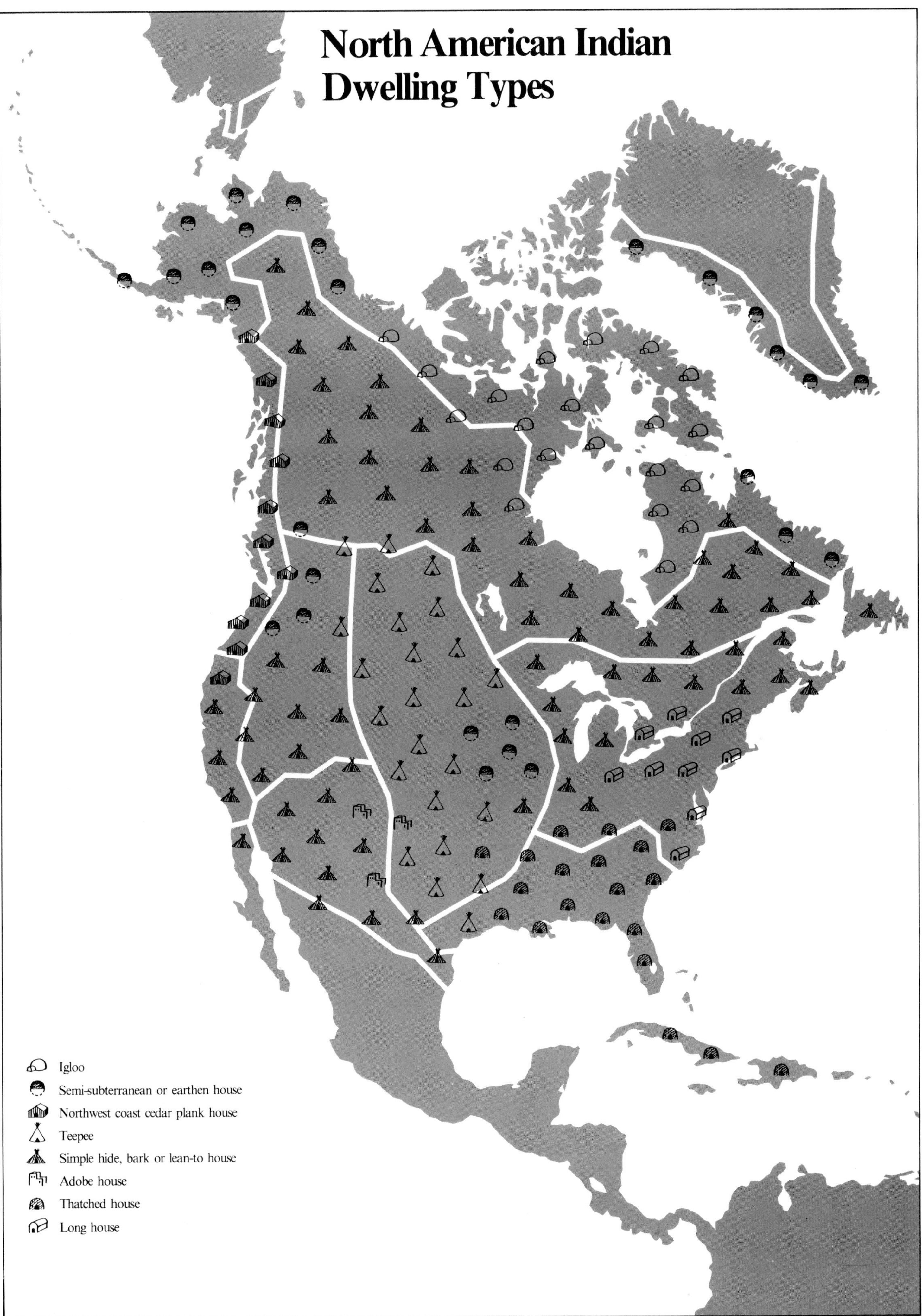
North American Indian
Dwelling Types
Igloo
Semi-subterranean or earthen house
Northwest coast cedar plank house
Teepee
Simple hide, bark or lean-to house
Adobe house
Thatched house
Long house

by the Zapotec Indians between 600 BC and 900 AD. They, too, built temples, tombs and pyramids and they designed some of the finest quality jewelry found in ancient North America.

The far corner of southeastern Mexico, the Yucatan, was the home of the most complex culture to develop in the Americas. The Mayan civilization came into existence around 1000 BC and reached its peak at between 300 and 900 AD in various centers, from Yucatan to Guatemala, Belize and Honduras. The community was run by priests and managed by nobles who lived in luxury. The Mayans achieved great heights of intellectual and artistic creativity —they constructed large temple pyramids, devised a primitive alphabet and developed an intricate calendar based on the stars. They loved decoration and covered their bodies with paint and tattooed designs. Eventually conflicts

Left: Relics of copper implements from Wisconsin. The Indians of the Mississippi Valley mound-building culture were skilled metalworkers and made tools, weapons, ornaments and utensils by pounding the copper that was so abundant around the Great Lakes. Those Indians who lived far from the mines were faced with the laborious task of making the long journey to and from the site, mining the metal for months at a time and then hauling the cumbersome loads back to their home territory on foot, the primary mode of transportation at that time.

Above: The Calendar Stone, one of the great monuments of the Aztec culture, was sculpted in the year 1479 for the festival of the sun on the orders of the king of Mexico. The stone was hauled by thousands of workers overground from the quarry to the pyramid, where the calendar was to reside. The 24-ton disk is nearly 12 feet in diameter. In its center is the decorated face of the sun god, surrounded by the symbols for earth, air, water and fire. Precise subdivisions show 20 days to the month. Eighteen months plus five unlucky days make up a 365-day year. The calendar was buried in 1521 in order to avoid total destruction by the conquistadores. In 1790 it was unearthed and later incorporated into the wall of the cathedral of Mexico City, where it now resides as a testament to the skills and contributions of these early peoples.

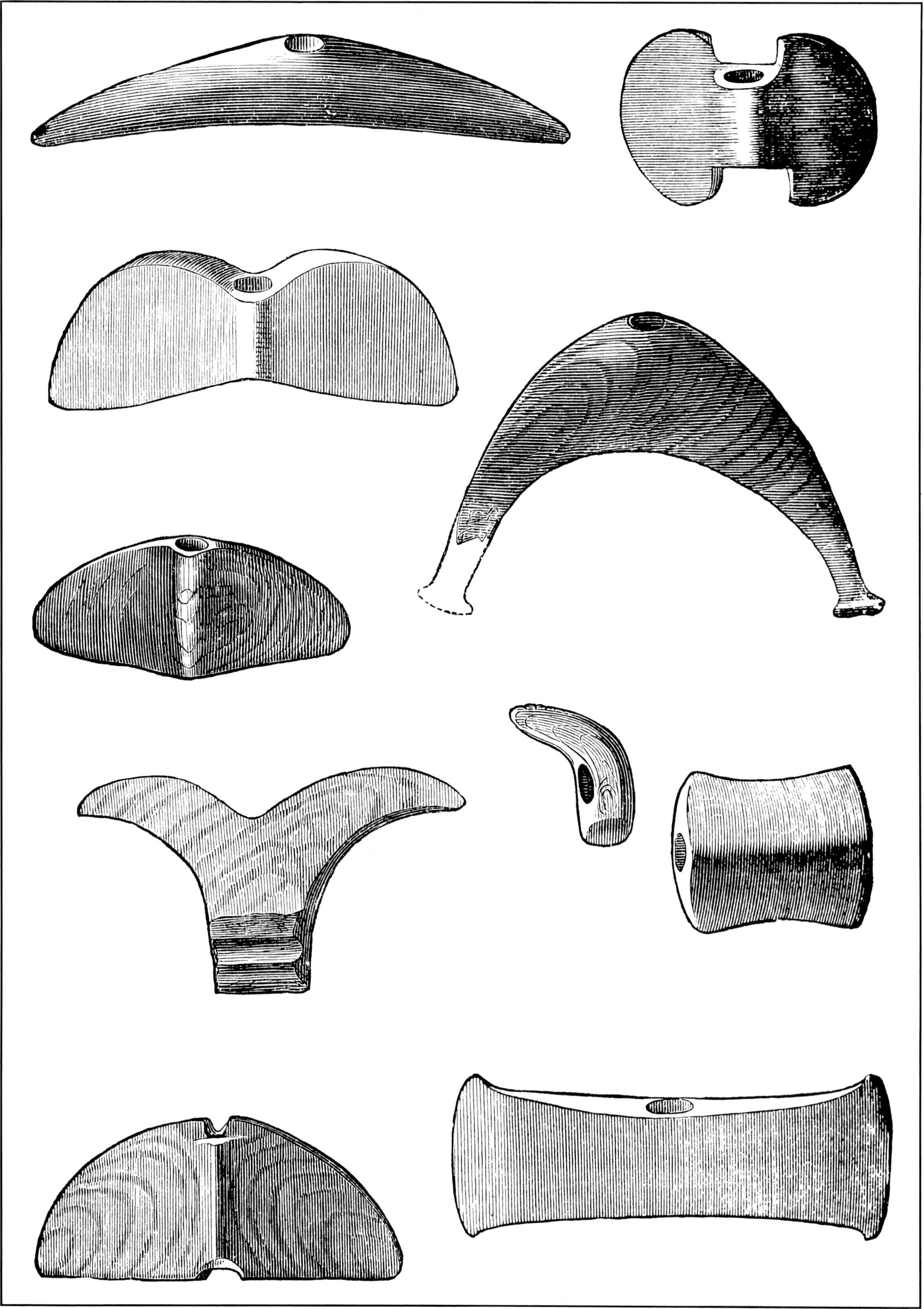

Left: The smooth surface of these drilled ceremonial weapons was achieved by a process of abrading and grinding them. Soft stone, like slate, was easy to drill using other stones as bores. Such decorative pieces have been found in the Mississippi Valley mounds, where they were buried along with the dead.

Above: The Aztecs regularly sacrificed plants and animals to the gods. During ceremonies like this one for the sun god, humans were also sacrificed and their flesh eaten. The cultures of Mesoamerica evolved numerous and elaborate rituals in order to stay in the gods' good favor.

developed which brought about its downfall.

Yet another extravagant culture developed at Teotihuacan in the Valley of Mexico, near Mexico City, around 200 BC. The community was a large-scale, intricately planned metropolis, run by a central government. Manufacturing and trade gave rise to great prosperity. Huge temples and individual apartments lined primitive streets that provided for irrigation and sewage. When this civilization fell into decline around 700 AD, the warlike Toltec Indians flourished in Central Mexico. In addition to being the first true architects and builders, they were the first Indians to work in gold and silver.

The last of the great Mesoamerican civilizations was introduced into the valley around 1200 AD by the Aztecs. They developed a highly ordered and powerful military society that ruled by conquest for 300 short years. They established a far-reaching trade route and controlled most of central Mexico. By that time the Indian population in Mesoamerica had climbed to a grand 15 million. When Hernando Cortez reached the Aztec capital of Tenochtitlan in 1519, Montezuma II was king and there was a great deal of discord in the conquered lands. With neighboring Indians as allies, the Spanish overthrew the Aztec leaders and destroyed the capital city, obliterating the glorious Indian civilization in 1521. Having achieved this, the Spanish conquistadores then turned their attention northward, to the vast promising land of North America.

In North America the advent of farming brought about cultural changes of enormous proportions, and this marked the beginning of the Formative Period of Indian cultural development. Between 1000 BC and 1000 AD, North American Indians reached the pinnacle of their civilization. The demands of planting and harvesting crops forced them to become more ordered in daily life. They became territorial and developed a village life, complete with political organizations and complex religious concepts. They were flexible in adapting to changes in climate and in the evolution of animal life, developing new skills such as pottery and basketmaking along the way. Although some Indians remained essentially nomadic, by 500 AD most were raising crops like corn, squash and beans.

The influences of the great Mesoamerican civilizations spread north over a period of time and were felt in places like the Southwest as well as the Mississippi Valley, where the new ideas and practices were incorporated into diverse cultural communities. Altogether nine distinct cultural areas evolved in North America, all confined within geographical limits: the Arctic, Subarctic, Northwest Coast, California, Great Basin, Southwest, Plains and Prairies, Northeast and Southeast. By the time the first Europeans arrived on this continent, an estimated two and one half million Indians, organized into 600 tribes, populated North America. Each had its own customs and language and each had its own story to tell.

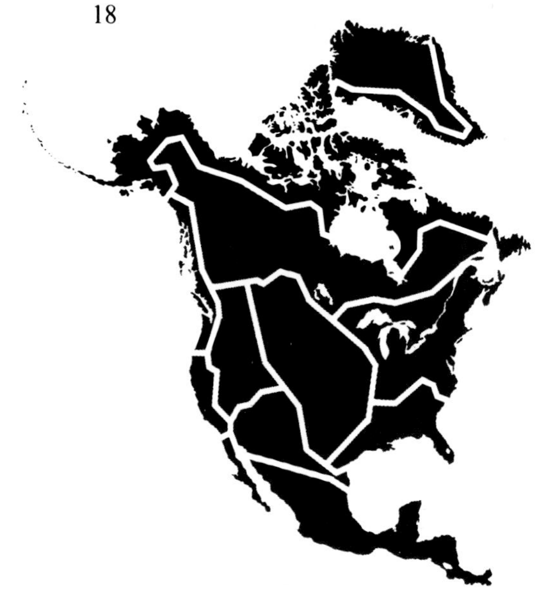

INDIANS OF THE ARCTIC

Below: Eskimos in Point Barrow, Alaska in 1935 prepare to haul an umiak. This open boat was constructed out of seal or walrus skins stretched over a whalebone frame and waterproofed with seal oil. Umiaks are very lightweight but are extremely sturdy and maneuverable in icy waters and capable of carrying huge loads, such as whales. This type of boat is still used today, although the paddles have been replaced with motors.

Right: An Eskimo woman in front of her skin-covered summer hut. Most Eskimos today live in permanent settlements, but in the past tribes dispersed in the spring and traveled inland in search of food.

On the inhospitable northern fringes of the North American continent, live a unique people whose land and culture stretch for 6000 miles across the shores of the Arctic Ocean through some of the most rugged territory in the world. The people are called Eskimo, meaning eaters of raw flesh, a name given them by the Algonquians to the south, but they refer to themselves as Inuit, which simply means "the people." In other areas of the continent an area as vast as that populated by the Eskimo would be home to tribes speaking a multitude of languages, probably even from several linguistic groups. Not so here. From eastern Siberia to the shores of Greenland, the Eskimo language is, with some minor local variations, the same. This is just one of the mysteries surrounding the Eskimo. Probably the biggest mystery is why they all live in so severe a climate at

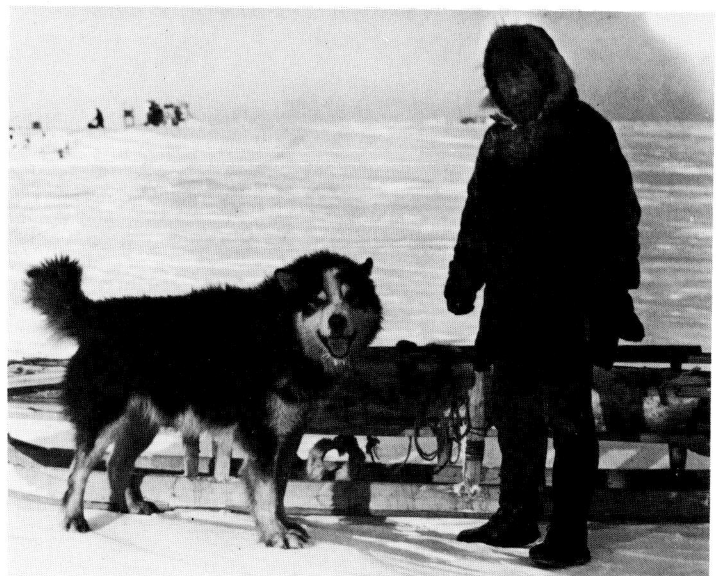

Above: A male Eskimo with a husky, his once indispensible companion. The thick-haired husky, the largest and strongest of all dogs put to domestic use by North American Indians, was capable of traveling at speeds up to 40 mph.

Below: The dog-drawn sled was the primary means of transport in the Arctic until the snow melted. The size of the dog team varied according to the load, and one lead dog took commands from the driver.

all. If the prevailing theory is correct, the ancestors of all Indians passed from Asia via the now long-gone Bering Land Bridge through central Alaska, through Eskimo country. When all the others passed through, why did the Eskimo stay on? Did they once migrate farther south and get driven north again by other tribes? Was there some event or belief, now hidden deep within their rich mythology, that caused them to settle in this white hell?

The answers to these questions will perhaps remain forever shrouded in the drifting snows of time and the Arctic, but we do know that there exists very solid archeological evidence that the ancestors of today's Eskimo were living in Alaska in 3000 BC. We also know a great deal about their way of life, which probably changed little in the nearly five millennia before the white man first mingled with these people on the barren windswept country north of Hudson Bay. The Eskimo's life is a continuous struggle against the natural forces of his environment, from the biting cold of the Arctic winter to the mosquitos of summer. But these people have adapted well, becoming as much an integral part of this harsh ecosystem as the seal and walrus upon whom they depend for their livelihood—more so than other birds and animals like gulls and foxes who are just seasonal visitors to the Far North.

When the long night of the Arctic winter descends upon the Far North, the Eskimo's life turns inward to small villages consisting of one-room houses. The Eskimo houses of Alaska and Siberia are usually semi-subterranean wood or earthen structures, but the inhabitants of northern Canada and the islands of the Arctic Ocean north of Hudson Bay often live in the traditional ice house called an igloo. The igloo can be surprisingly hospitable, kept warm by a small fire. Two entire related families might share a single igloo, remaining quite comfortable amid piles of polar bear and musk ox hides, spending long winter nights socializing in their compact home against the flicker of a whale-blubber-fueled soapstone lamp while the Arctic gale screams outside. The centerpiece of the winter village (in spring the families will go their separate ways for the summer months) is a ceremonial igloo where community festivities take place. Weddings, a traditional celebration in many cultures, will not take place here, however. An Eskimo marriage is an informal affair that usually involves a girl simply moving in with her intended in her mid-teens. Occasionally a marriage was arranged by the parents, because the practice of female infanticide (killing girl-babies) eventually reduced the number of eligible potential brides. An arranged marriage would ensure a wife for one's son.

Hunting during the winter is a difficult, though not insurmountable, chore. The seal is the staple game animal. Known as *puiji*, or those who show their noses, seals are hunted through the very holes through which they show their noses. Because it is a mammal, the seal must come up for air and is then vulnerable to the hunter. The traditional weapon was the spear, but nets were also used to set traps for the seal. In the last century more sophisticated harpoons as well as guns have appeared in the hunter's arsenal. While the men hunt, the women are occupied with such necessary chores as drying clothes, caring for the young children and chewing the family's boots to keep them supple.

Both whales and walrus are also important to the Eskimo, providing not only food but ivory for tools and ceremonial uses as well. In the spring and summer months, birds return to the Arctic and become part of the Eskimo diet.

While they winter along the shores of the Arctic Ocean, summer finds these hearty people many miles inland, where they construct elaborate systems of stone dams and channels in inland streams that enable them to take large numbers of salmon. These salmon, harvested on their annual northward migration to their spawning grounds, are eaten during the summer or dried and saved for the long lean winter. In the fall the caribou meat and hides are put to use.

Left: An Alaskan crow mask carved from wood. An abundance of demons and deities inhabited the Eskimo world and were significant aspects of their culture and daily life. During the long winter nights, men carved out crude masks representing the various spirits, who would be impersonated during ceremonies. The masks were usually carved out of driftwood, which was hard to find on the barren tundra, and designed under the direction of the shamans. The shaman was the intermediary between the real world and the spiritual world, and he was inspired by his visions. Straightforward masks representing animals were used for secular ceremonies.

During the ceremony itself the men wore the mask while they danced vigorously. Women wore small finger masks, often duplicates of those worn by the men, and danced behind the men in a gentle swaying fashion. For important ceremonial dances a large square drum suspended from the ceiling was played.

Men of the tribe made the drums and played them, and they also did most of the singing, an essential part of most ceremonies that served to invoke the appropriate spirit. Arguments between men were also carried out in a song duel. The two men sang insults and intimidations to each other, while the remaining adults looked on as jury.

Right: This abstract face mask from the Lower Yukon is one of the more famous creations of the Eskimos and is unusual for its asymmetrical design. Masks were the largest pieces of art that the Eskimos produced and many were painted in bright colors. Abstract masks, reserved for the religious ceremonies, were often very complex or obscure in design and their significance was understood only by the shaman who directed the project.

Below: A carved Eskimo artifact in the shape of a seal. The bulk of Eskimo art consisted of carvings, all of which were done by men. Simple tools were used to shape ivory, bone, horn or wood with great care and a delicate touch. The objects were often small and the simple designs were abstract, geometrical or representations of animals from daily life.

Eskimos were well known for the tiny figurines, toys and charms they turned out, and also for their skill and artistry in decorating everyday functional tools, weapons and utensils. Although many Eskimos lived on the edge of starvation, they all devoted resources to dance, decoration, carving and ritual, and to individual creativity.

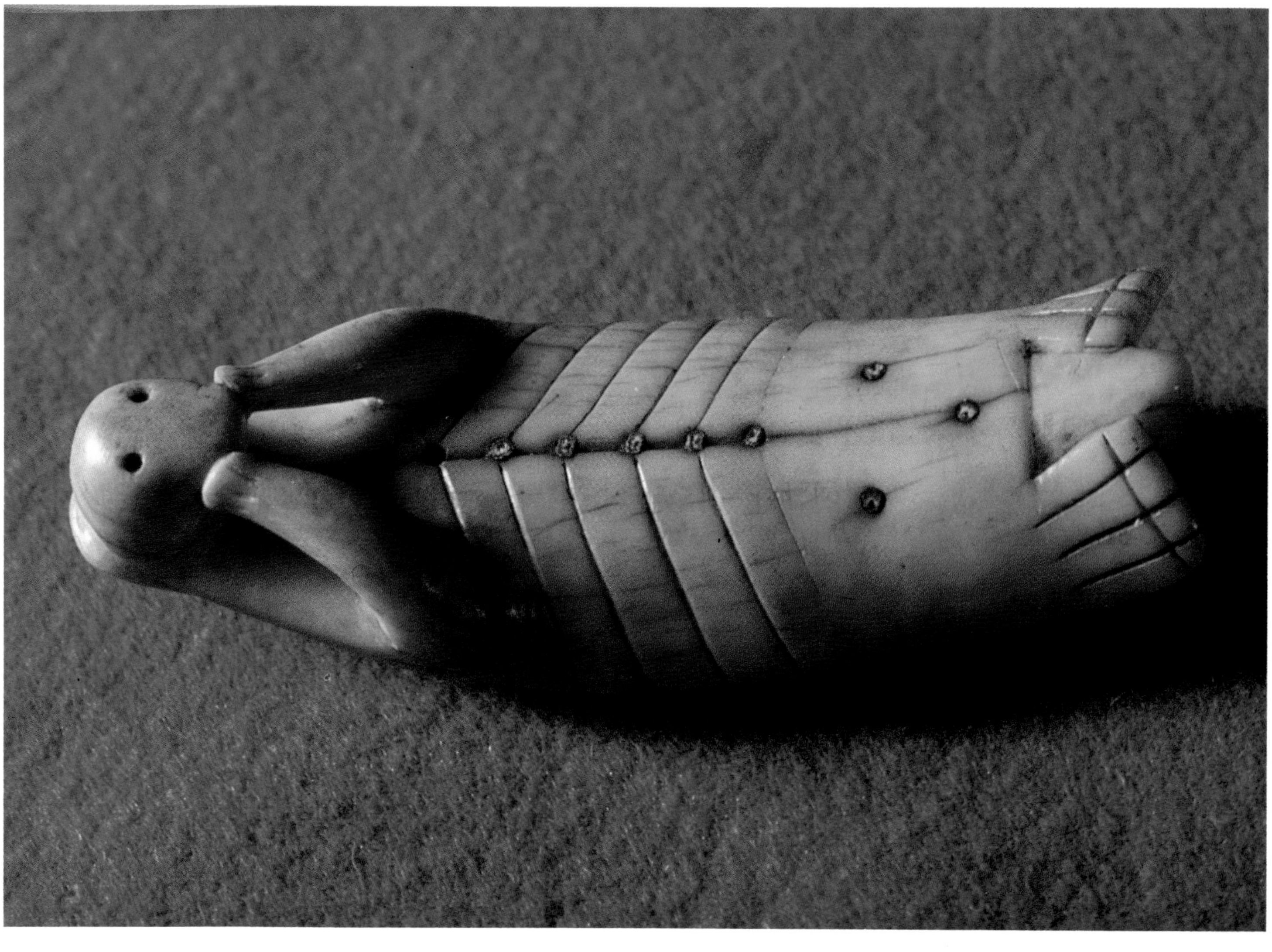

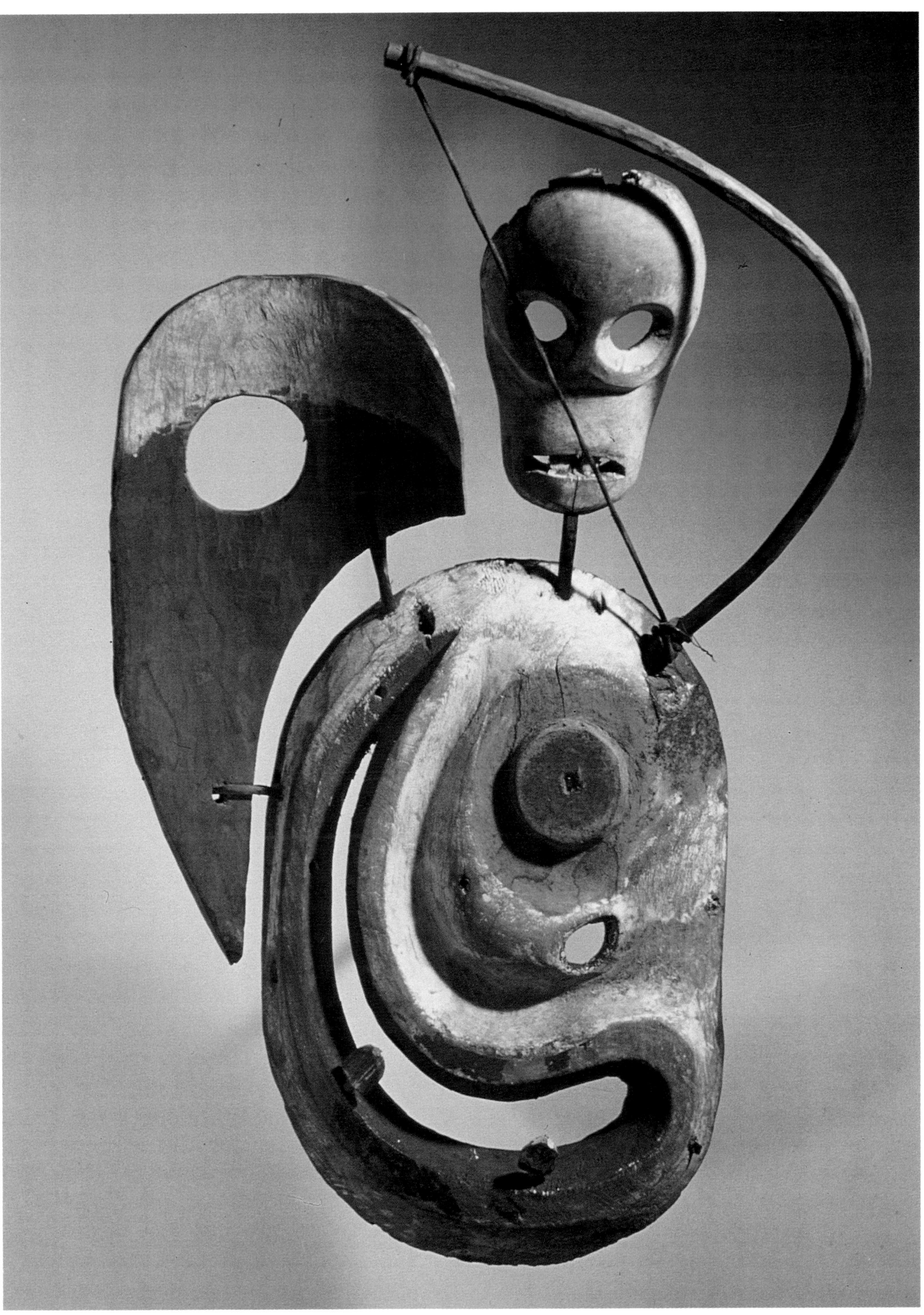

As means of transportation, in a land where the invention of the wheel would have been worthless, the Eskimos developed efficient dogsleds for travel across the frozen land and kayaks and umiaks for the rivers and sea. The kayak is a small, fast, one-person boat, similar to a canoe, whose design has even been borrowed by the white man. The umiak, a larger boat, carries a greater number of people and is used in whale hunting in the open sea.

The Eskimo is at home in the stark world of nature's extremes, but he also inhabits a supernatural world, filled with shadowy demons and ghosts. Few cultures have as strong a belief in the ethereal or such a high per-capita number of shamans, or medicine men. Demons lurk everywhere in the dark world of the Arctic winter, and while some may be benevolent, others are hostile and bloodthirsty. Souls of the dead live on as wicked spirits if proper rituals are not followed and taboos observed. Dietary laws are particularly important in the pantheon of beliefs. Mixing the flesh of land and sea animals is strictly forbidden.

When seals or whales are killed, they are ceremonially given a drink of water so that they will go back to the spirit world to report that they were treated with respect. Future seals or whales can then confidently allow themselves to be killed by the same hunter. A polar bear's spirit remains on the spear that has killed him for five days, so his skin must be kept inside for that time. The shamans who maintain the delicate balance between the natural and spirit worlds were once ordinary hunters who discovered along the way that they had a special gift of extraordinary powers. They were empowered to heal the sick by chasing away demons and by locating stolen souls, returning them to the bodies of their owners.

In contrast to what was happening to their cousins in more temperate climes, the Eskimos had little contact with the white man until the nineteenth century. The first contact was probably with the Norsemen in Greenland, but few Eskimos on the North American continent had seen white men until the Hudson Bay Company trappers made their way north in the eighteenth century. Within the next hundred years the traders exchanged guns, knives and whisky for furs and ivory, but the traditional lifestyle remained largely intact. Gradually the use of firearms, more reliable than spears, cut deeply into the stock of wild game, and the religion of the missionaries mixed with the shamanism of earlier times. However, even as the way of life changed in those areas of Alaska where the white man established *his* villages, the old ways held fast in the remote areas.

Above: Alaskan Eskimos harpoon a whale. The dangerous whale hunt takes place in the spring when the ice begins to break up. The hunters thrust the harpoon into the animal to wound it and secure it, and then they kill it with spears. When it is dead, the hunting party hauls it back to the camp, where it is beheaded. The whale hunt traditionally was surrounded by ceremony, and at this point the wife of the captain would offer water to the head as a mark of respect to its spirit to encourage more whales to come to their hunting grounds.

Right: The Eskimos used a variety of weapons for hunting. The spear on the left is used in conjunction with an atlatl, or thrower, for catching fish and birds. The atlatl allows the hunter to maintain more distance between himself and his prey and to increase the momentum of the spear. It is attached to the spear by a long line of rawhide. The two harpoons to the right are used for hunting walruses. The removable head remains in the body of the animal and is attached to the spear by a long flexible line. The spear is then used like a fishing pole to retrieve the prey.

Left: An Eskimo spear and fish-shaped lure. The lure is dangled in the water to attract the fish. The spear, called a leisler, is used to recover the fish. The central prong pierces the fish and the two prongs hold the fish in place to keep it from escaping. Fishing with a spear is most effective in shallow water or in weirs built to trap large numbers of fish. The prongs are carved out of musk ox antlers and the sharp prong out of bone. The lure, typically, has been decorated in a delicate pattern.

Above: Carved wooden snow goggles protect against sun blindness.

Below: The construction of a snowhouse, or igloo, could be completed in about an hour. The domed snowhouse is the temporary winter home of Eskimos who live in the central Arctic only. Large blocks of hardened snow are cut and stacked in circular rows around the builder. When the walls are completed, he finishes by cutting out the ventilation hole and the entrance.

Left: An Eskimo mother with her child, photographed around 1915. Women carried their babies in slings under their parka or in their hoods for warmth. An amulet attached to the parka was endowed with magical properties that would protect the child. Eskimos loved children and treated them with a great deal of patience and affection, rarely inflicting any type of punishment on them. A wife's value was determined by her ability to produce children as well as by her skill at household tasks.

Female infanticide was commonly practiced by some Eskimos, mainly in the central Arctic, out of sheer necessity when times were difficult and food supplies were short. At times like these, boys were more valued because they would become hunters and supply food. After the father made the decision to kill his infant daughter, the mother carried out the act by suffocating the child or letting it freeze to death. Child betrothal was also common; since the female population was small, the young boy could be guaranteed a wife. Betrothed female infants were exempt from infanticide. Because life in the Arctic was difficult, children learned early to accept the responsibilities of an adult. Young girls helped their mothers with household chores and in caring for younger children. They usually married shortly after reaching puberty. Young boys spent much of their time with their father and by the age of 10 began to hunt. A pregnant woman was considered unclean and was isolated for the duration of her pregnancy. She delivered the child herself, and for the year following the birth, her diet and eating hours were strictly regulated. A new mother was permitted to eat only the cooked meat of the animals that had been killed by her husband.

Below: An Alaskan Eskimo dance orchestra pounds drums made from whale stomachs stretched over a hoop. These single-headed flat, tambourine-like drums are the only type of musical instrument in the Arctic and they accompany all singing.

Things did not go as well for the Arctic's other native tribe, the Aleuts. A more recent transplant from the Asian mainland, the Aleuts settled on the chain of rocky islands extending westward from Alaska that today bears their name. Because they were island dwellers, they were less nomadic than the Eskimos and tended to build larger and more elaborate wooden houses similar to those of the Indians of the Northwest Coast. Originally slave-keepers themselves, they were enslaved by the Russians when the latter occupied the Aleutian Islands in the mid-eighteenth century. Over the course of the next century, 80 percent of the Aleutian population was decimated by the Russians. When Alaska and the Aleutians became US territory in 1867, the population had declined to barely 2000, from which it has increased less than one fold.

Ironically, in the present day of global tension between the United States and the Soviet Union, the distance of open water or solid ice separating the two superpowers in this region is barely two miles. Both Eskimo and Aleut cultures span this icy artificial border and these native people are generally able to slip across it as easily as the seals, the walrus or the Arctic fox.

Above: An Eskimo dog team pulls a sled across the snow. In the eastern Arctic huskies were each harnessed to their own line and they drew the sled in a fan formation, with the lead dog in the middle. In the western Arctic dogs were attached in pairs to one line, with the lead dog at the front, and they drew the sled in single file.

Below: A tiny ivory carving of a dog team and sled.

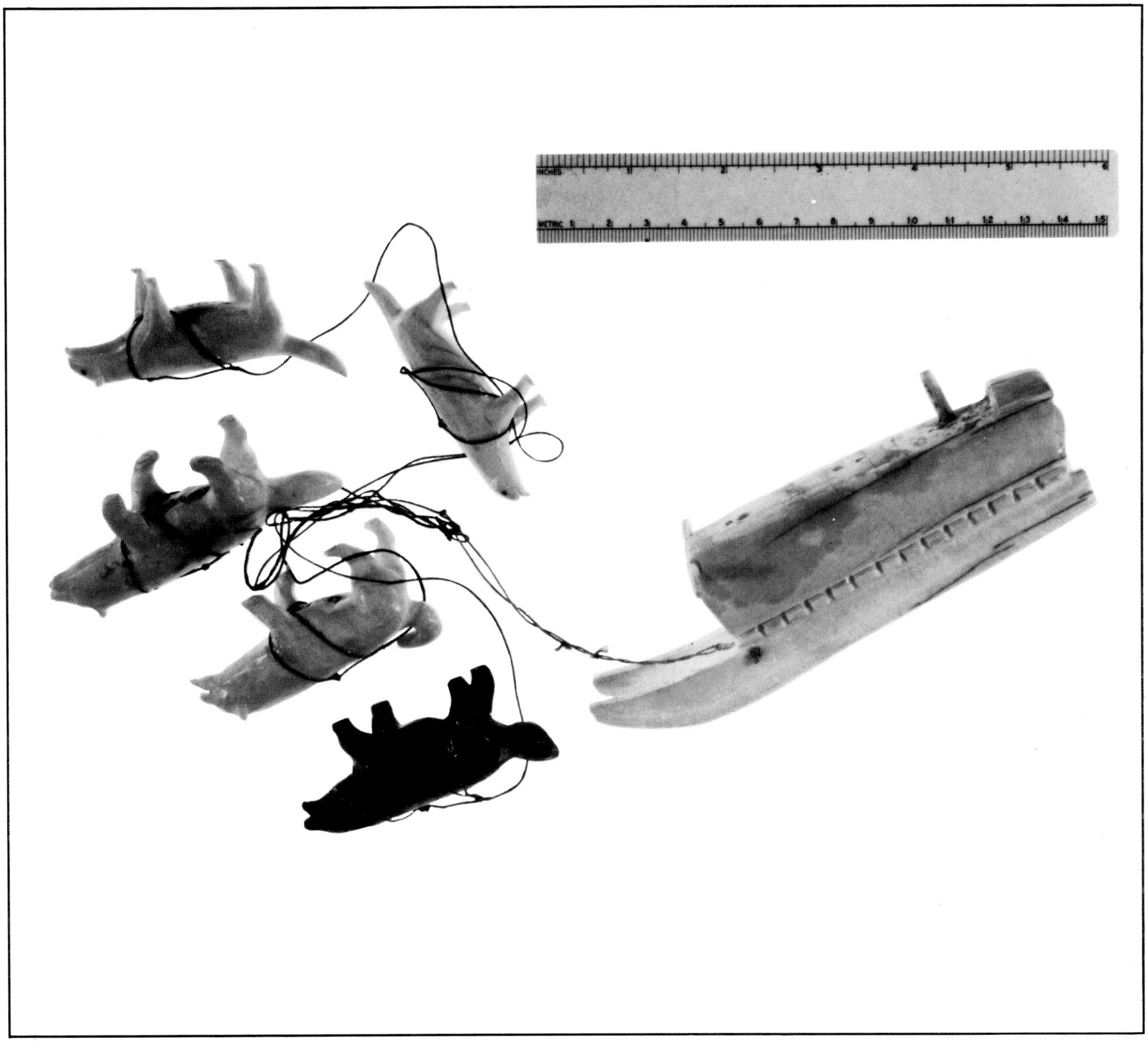

INDIANS OF THE SUBARCTIC

Below the continent's frozen northern tier are the vast flat steppes of northern Canada and central Alaska. This immense tundra, scraped bare by the enormous glaciers of the ice age, is the home of the peoples of two distinct linguistic groups. To the west are the Athabaskans (Athapaskans) of central Alaska and the areas of northern Canada west of Hudson Bay. To the south and east of Hudson Bay are the Algonquian-speaking peoples, who are related to those of the same linguistic groups living farther to the south, around the Great Lakes.

The lifestyles of two peoples could not have been more different. For the Athabaskans, of whom the major tribes were the Chipewyans, Digrib (Thlingchadinne) and Hare (Kawchodinneh), everything was geared toward mere subsistence, and the key element to that subsistence was the caribou. Other game (moose and bighorn sheep included) were important, but the caribou was central to

Below: Athabaskan hunters outside their camp with a sled load of recently killed mountain sheep.

Right: In the Subarctic caribou provided most necessities of life for the people of this harsh world.

Indian Tribes of the Subarctic

Abittibi	**Eyak**	**Naskapi**
Ahtena	**Hare**	**Slave**
Beaver	**Ingalik**	**Tanaina**
Beothuk	**Kaska**	**Tanana**
Carrier	**Koyukon**	**Tutchone**
Chipewyan	**Kutchin**	**Yellowknife**
Cree	**Montagnais**	
Dogrib	**Mountain**	

Athabaskan existence. It is theorized that these people followed the caribou migration across the Bering Land Bridge and first arrived in this region in 10,000 BC. Indeed, the nomadic life would continue for most Athabaskans well into the twentieth century. The annual arrival of the caribou herds was the year's high point. Once slain, the caribou were eaten boiled and then preserved for future use in a dried, powdered form known as pemmican (the Cree word for dried meat). The dog was an equally important animal. Dogs had been domesticated early in the prehistory of mankind throughout North America and around the world, but they were so highly regarded by the Athabaskans that they were considered to be man's brother. Dog sleds, similar to those used by the Eskimo, became an important means of transportation for the Athabaskans.

The overwhelming need to address the matter of subsistence gave the Athabaskans little time to develop the elaborate religious life that evolved elsewhere on the continent. The presence of demons and other specters from the spirit world was perceived and the role of shamans developed to deal with them. The Athabaskans lived far enough south to not have the long dark winters of virtual hibernation many Eskimos experienced but too far north to enjoy any respite from a harsh and bitter climate. This climate which gave the people no spare time to develop religion also affected the development of their social life. The tribal system was not nearly as important as it was farther south, and chiefs existed only to serve as natural leaders who simply took charge when the situation demanded someone to do so.

The Algonquians lived a virtually pastoral existence by comparison with their Athabaskan brothers. These people, predominantly the various Cree tribes and the Ojibwa (Chippewa), lived in the vast boreal forests north of the Great Lakes. They subsisted on such delicacies as wild rice and maple sugar, fished the rivers that flowed through their territory and hunted the deer that populated these rich forests. In the summer these people could be found camped in the sugar maple groves in the southern part of their range, tanning hides and building canoes. The Athabaskans also had canoes, but they were shorter than the bark canoes constructed by the Algonquians of the Subarctic and the Northeast.

The Algonquians were the first people of the Subarctic to encounter the white man, though the Algonquians of the Northeast had several centuries of interaction with these strange people from across the great water before the latter made their presence felt in the Subarctic. The first European traders made their way into the region in the middle of the seventeenth century, and guns and iron kettles became part of Indian life. It was not until the beginning of the twentieth century, though, that a concentrated network of trading posts was established in the Subarctic. A treaty, providing for government social services in exchange for Indian land, was signed between the Canadian government and the Ojibwa and Cree in 1905, but it was not until 1930 that similar treaties were extended to other tribes. By 1940 boarding schools were established to educate the Indian children, bringing them from far-flung parts of the Subarctic to concentrated sites where both their schooling and health care could be conveniently administered by the government. By 1960 the old ways had virtually disappeared in the Algonquian regions, and it was only in the far north of Canada, on the vast steppes that had helped create the Athabaskan way of life, that this way of life lingered on.

Above: Two Ojibwa children from Minnesota in the 1930s. At the beginning of the spring the Ojibwas left their winter camp and headed for summer villages near the maple sugar groves.

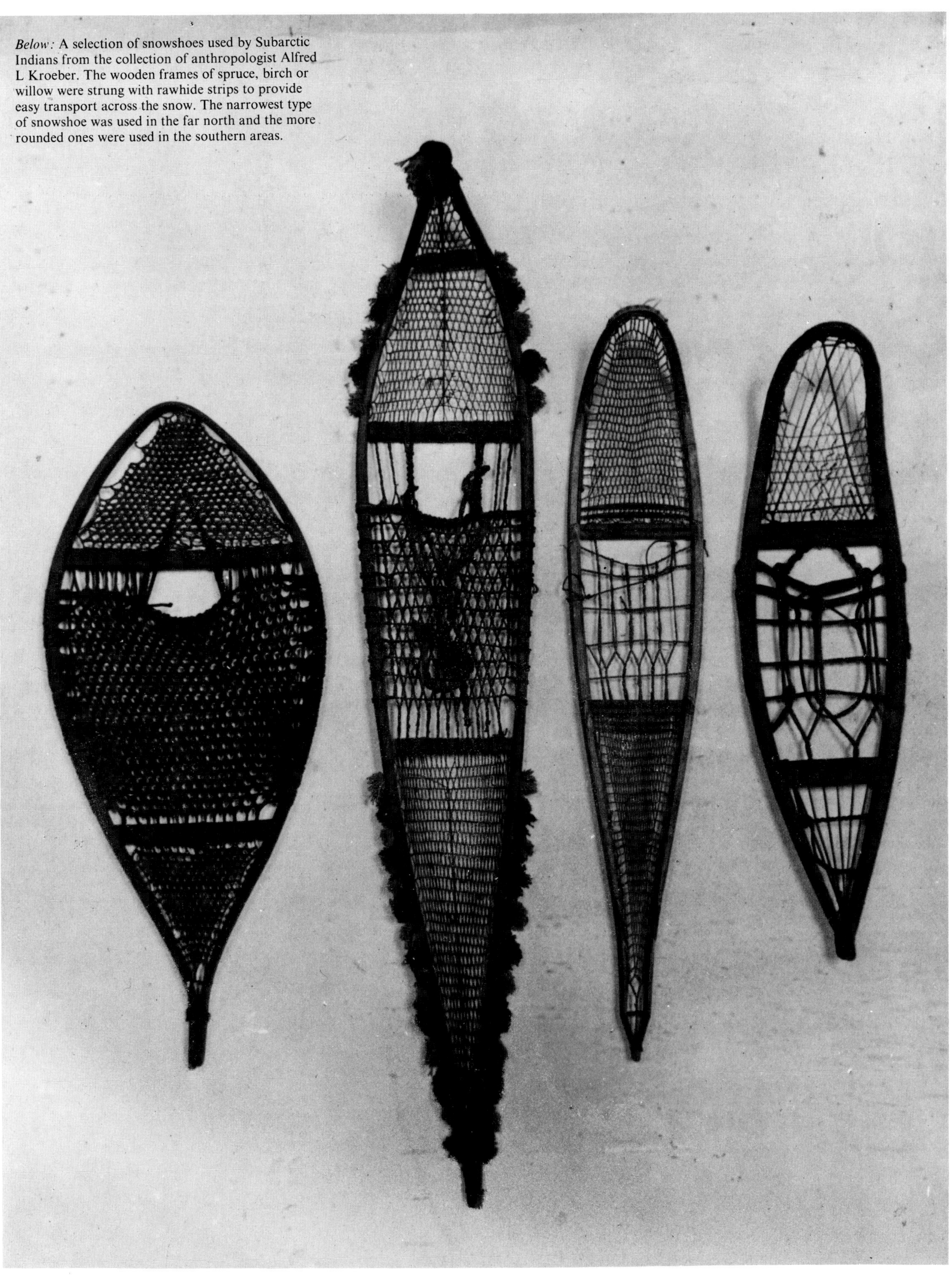

Below: A selection of snowshoes used by Subarctic Indians from the collection of anthropologist Alfred L Kroeber. The wooden frames of spruce, birch or willow were strung with rawhide strips to provide easy transport across the snow. The narrowest type of snowshoe was used in the far north and the more rounded ones were used in the southern areas.

It had been changed forever by flannel shirts and Winchesters, and by canned goods and battery-operated radios, but these changes seemed to mark only another turn in the natural evolution of these tribes, like the domestication of the dog centuries ago. Today the Athabaskan still follows the caribou on a vast unfenced land.

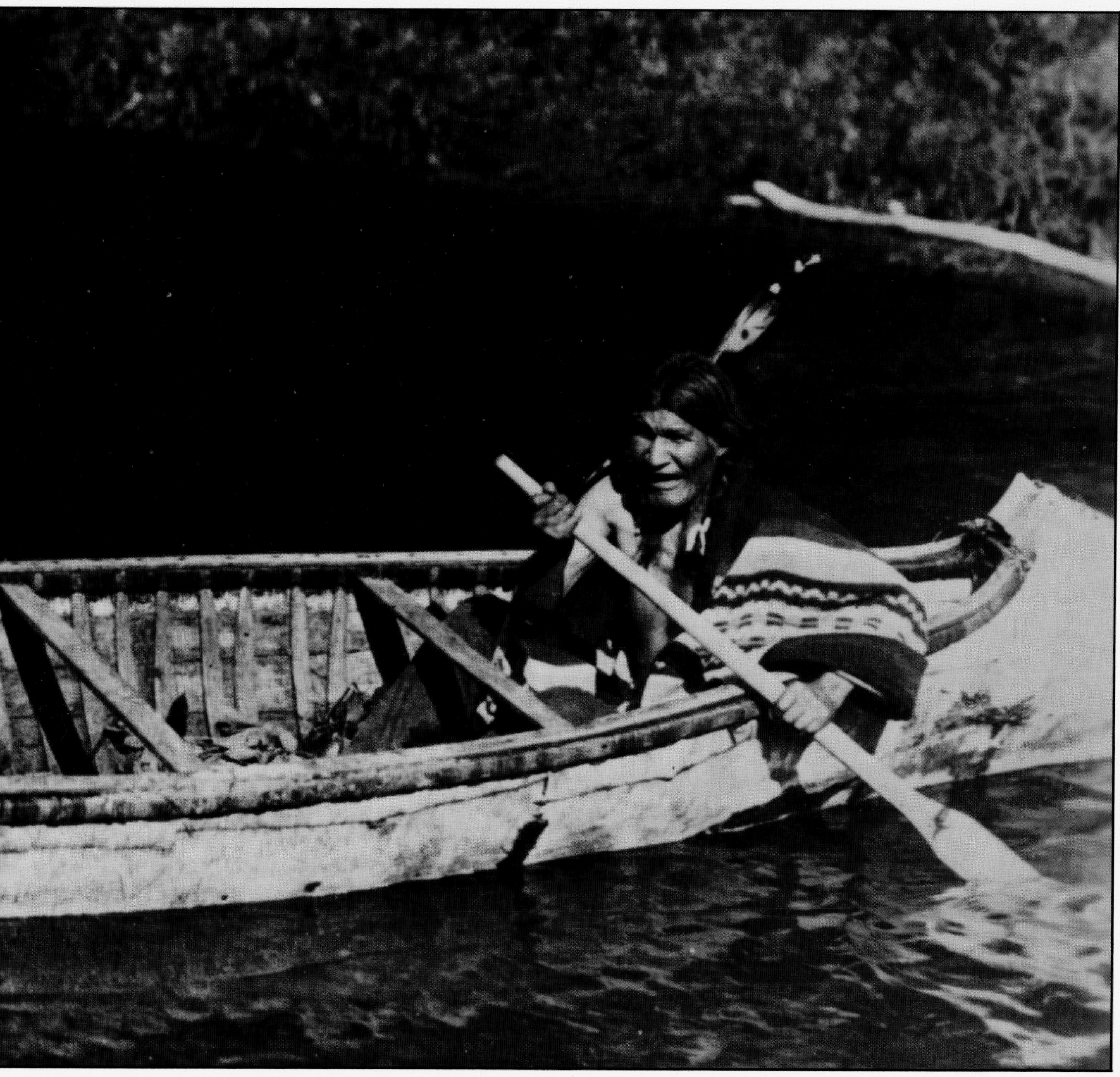

The Canoe Builders of the Subarctic

Above: Chippewa hunters in their indispensible birchbark canoe. An extensive network of lakes and rivers in the Subarctic made travel by water a major mode of transportation by the Indians, and they became skilled boatmakers. A variety of styles evolved depending on the materials available in the local area, and in the north the predominant type was the birchbark canoe.

Of all types of boats built in North America by the Indians, the umiak, kayak and birchbark canoe were superior in construction and quality. The Chippewas were hunters, not farmers, and consequently were usually on the move. The canoe was a versatile and sturdy piece of equipment for them. It was strong but lightweight and could be easily carried overground. Turned upside down, it provided good protection from the elements. Over water it was essential for trading, hunting and for general travel.

Construction of a canoe required about two weeks of intensive work, which was usually carried out in the springtime. The men cut the wood and the bark while the women did the sewing. Bark was removed from white birch trees in huge sheets and sewn inside-out onto a white cedar frame with spruce or pine root "threads" that were soaked in water for flexibility. Pine gum was heated and mixed with fat to seal the seams and the floor was strengthened with sheets of cedar.

Chippewa canoes were short—only about 13 feet long—and widest at the rear. Variations in the shape of the structure were based on the type of water to be travelled; high bows and sterns were more efficient in rugged waters and low bows and sterns were appropriate for quiet waters.

In this photograph by Roland Reed, one Indian propels and guides the canoe with the paddle made out of hard maple wood, while the hunter with the bow and arrow takes aim on his prey.

Left: A Passamaquoddy man builds a canoe with the help of his wife and child in this photo taken in 1875. After the wooden gunwale was tied together with pine roots, it was placed on the white side of a huge sheet of birchbark and weighed down.

The bark that would become the sides of the canoe was split and held upright by stakes pounded into the ground. These were tied together at the top to hold the upper frame in place. The gunwales were lifted and sewn to the frame tied by the stakes to the top of the boat. It was then turned upside down for the bottom edges to be sewn and for the resin to be applied. The man in this photograph is shown in the last stage of construction. He is lining the inside of the canoe lengthwise with strips of cedar. These are held in place by cross ribs, which are placed on top to provide additional strength. During construction the bark is kept wet to maintain flexibility, but when complete the canoe is sturdy and watertight.

Left: In Minnesota, *circa* 1925 a Chippewa woman ties wild rice, one of the chief foods of the area. The woman established a claim to her portion of the rice by going out 10 days before harvest time and tying portions of stalks in small sheaves. When the rice was ripe she untied the sheaves and beat the rice out with a paddle. It was then dried out in the sun or over a low fire.

Below: A Chippewa bark teepee at Red River, Canada in 1858. A frame of sapling poles was tied loosely at the top and covered with sheets of birchbark and reeds at the base. Teepees were the typical homes of nomadic Indians and in some regions were covered with skins. The conical shape of the teepee distinguishes it from the similar but dome-shaped wigwam.

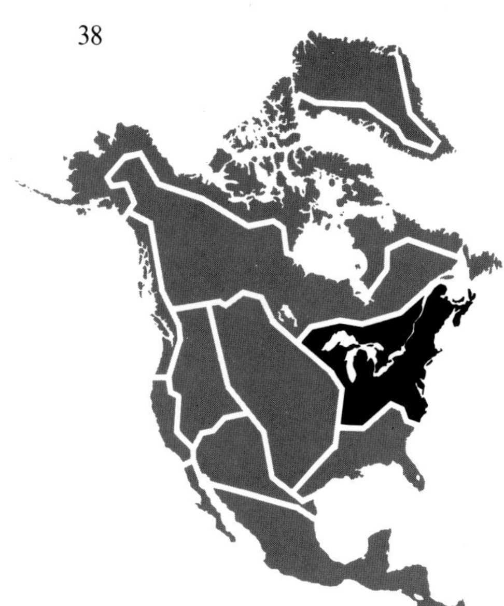

INDIANS OF THE NORTHEAST

The dense woodland that stretched from the Atlantic coast to the Mississippi River and from northern present-day Tennessee to the St Lawrence Valley took in the rocky coastlines, fertile coastal meadows and an abundance of mountains, rivers, and streams that supported a rich variety of plant and animal life. The Northeast was an expanse that was also endowed with a changeable climate and a wide range of temperatures. From about 10,000 to 7000 BC, when the climate was still harsh and disagreeable, this area was occupied first by the mammoth hunters and then by small-game hunters. By about 500 BC a distinct woodland culture had begun to develop and within 2000 years it reached its peak. In the middle of the 1500s the

Below: With the help of an Indian guide, Captain Miles Standish leads the first Puritan settlers over the embankment at Plymouth in the Massachusetts Bay Colony. Like Captain John Smith of Virginia, Standish was a leader with great military experience and he understood how to handle the Indians. He befriended Massasoit, Chief of the Wampanoags, and benefitted from a treaty with him that was made following the deaths of large numbers of his tribe due to new diseases. With this pact Massasoit granted the settlers a sizable piece of land. Cynics believe that Smith made up the story of being saved by Pocahontas.

Indian population in the Northeast stood at about 500,000.

The numerous Northeastern tribes had much in common. They were primarily farmers and hunters, they were superior warriors, and the women played a key role in daily life. Of all the tribes in North America they were the most advanced politically, and many merged into confederations as a means of dealing with mutual problems. They were also united by language. The three major language groups were Iroquoian, Siouan and Algonquian, the latter incorporating the largest number of Indians and covering the most territory. The Iroquoian-speaking Indians of the Northeast resided in the area of Upstate New York, between the Hudson Valley and Lake Erie. The Winnebago tribe in Wisconsin was the only member of the Siouan-language family, which prevailed on the Plains. The Algonquians were widespread over most of the Northeast.

The Iroquoian culture evolved in the north around 1300 AD and consisted of a group of hostile tribes that were in a constant state of war, trying to settle ever-increasing scores against each other. Like most Indians of North America, they were preoccupied with war and the art of warfare. The Iroquois, however, were similar to the Comanches in their voracity for it, and they were notorious for the terror they inflicted on their enemies—usually the Algonquians or dissident Iroquois tribes. Their greatest achievement was

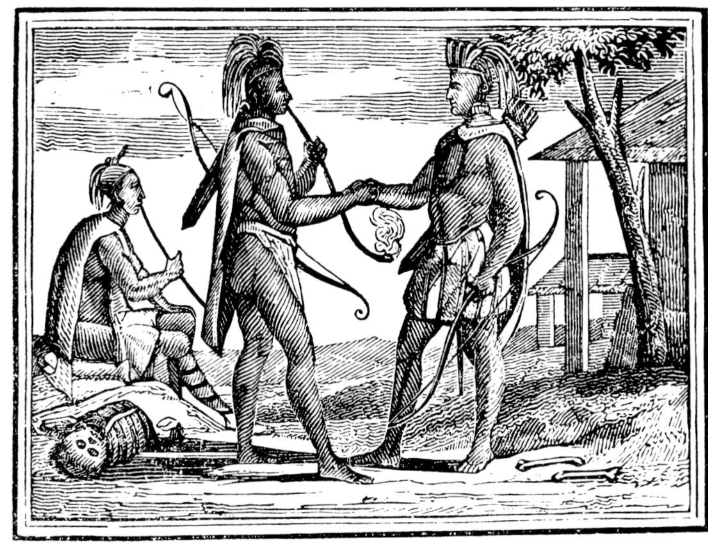

Above: Settlers in New England feared the alliances that were made among various Indian tribes. After 30 years of minor hostilities, Philip, successor to Massasoit, tired of harassment by white settlers and was determined to drive them out. He spent several years establishing a confederation of tribes in preparation for war against the colonists. Philip was killed in 1678, and the Wampanoags and their Narragansett allies were finally defeated two years later in the conclusion of King Philip's War. Few Indians remained in New England after this. Hundreds of the defeated Indians were sent as slaves to the West Indies, including Philip's wife and child.

Indian Tribes of the Northeast

Abnaki
Algonquian
Chickahominy
Chippewa
Delaware (Lenni-Lenape)
Erie
Fox
Huron
Illinois
Iroquois
  Cayuga
  Conestoga
  Mohawk
  Oneida
  Onondaga
  Seneca
Kickapoo
Mahican
Malecite
Massachuset
Mattapony
Menominee
Miami
Micmac
Missisauga
Mohegan
Montauk
Nanticoke
Narraganset
Neutral
Nipissing
Ottawa
Pamaunkey
Passamaquoddy
Pennacook
Penobscot
Pequod
Piankashaw
Poktumtuk
Potawatomi
Powhatan
Sauk
Secotan
Shawnee
Shinnecock
Susquehannock
Tobacco
Tuscarora
Wampanoag
Wappinger
Winnebago
Wyandot

the creation of the League of Iroquois (or Five Nations), the result of the famous chief Hiawatha's ambition to end the self-destruction of the Iroquois and to promote peace. The confederation was made up of the five major tribes, the Mohawks, Senecas, Oneidas, Onondagas and Cayugas, a formidable combined force. Iroquois territory was divided into five strips, and each tribe governed its territory by a council. Mutual problems and major issues were resolved

by the Great Council, a body of 49 representatives from the five tribes. The fiftieth seat was reserved for Hiawatha.

Iroquoian society was based on descent through the maternal line, and women dominated in this tribe more than in any other matrilineal Indian society. They oversaw all activities of the Great Council, although the men made decisions. They also looked after the inheritance of council seats. In the Seneca tribe the clan mother and older

Above: Early American woodcuts illustrated Indian attacks on colonists, common occurrences in the Northeast. Relations with the early settlers were often good, and the New England Indians helped them survive the first difficult years. Indians remained friendly while the white population was small and as long as settlers did not intrude excessively on their hunting territory. As colonies prospered, disputes arose over land and Indians were faced with the choice of surrendering their land or perishing.

Left: Corporal George, a Winnebago from Tomah, Wisconsin, stands with his rifle on guard duty for the US Army Signal Corps in Germany in 1919.

Above: The Pilgrims were startled when Samoset, a Wampanoag chief, walked out of the woods and greeted them in understandable English.

Below: In 1697 Indians attacked the town of Haverhill, Massachusetts and abducted Hannah Dustin, her week-old child and nurse. After her abductors killed her baby for crying, Mrs. Dustin waited for an appropriate moment and killed all but two of her small captive party. She saved the scalps and received a 25-pound reward on her return, when she was acclaimed a heroine.

Right: Benjamin West painted this portrait of Colonel Guy Johnson in 1776 now hanging in the National Gallery in Washington, D.C. Johnson succeeded Sir William Johnson, his father-in-law, as Superintendent of Indian Affairs for the English Crown from 1774 to 1782. In this capacity he was responsible for all Indian tribes, particularly the powerful Iroquois, whose loyalty he was able to maintain on behalf of the British throughout the Revolutionary War. His headquarters were based in Niagara, and from there he discharged raiding parties against the colonists.

women selected, and had power to dismiss, the eight tribal chiefs. The oldest woman of a clan ranked highest. After marriage, the man moved to the longhouse of his wife; all property belonged to her. Women bore their children in the woods away from the longhouse and were responsible for raising them, since the men were usually at war or hunting. When boys reached puberty, they were initiated into manhood after proving their courage by hurling themselves against rocks to draw blood. The ritual took place in the presence of an old man of the clan, whose job was to identify the boy's guardian spirit.

The Iroquois set up their villages at the forks of river or streams and erected a palisade or a moat for protection. Fields for crops surrounded the village. The community consisted of randomly arranged longhouses, one for each clan and with the clan crest painted above the door. The longhouse, a rectangular structure with an arched roof, was constructed of poles and sheets of bark. Inside, the walls were lined with two levels of bunks, one for sleeping and one for storing family possessions. Several fires were kept burning continuously.

The Iroquois world was governed by many supernatural beings. Ceremonies were a regular feature of their lives, and many were extended and elaborate affairs. One of the most important was the four-day-long Great Corn Festival for giving thanks for the corn harvest. During the

Above: The Cambridge-educated Roger Williams was a radical who preached the separation of church and state in Salem, Massachusetts. When ordered to return to England, he fled to Rhode Island in 1636 where he founded Providence. He also preached tolerance and developed a friendly relationship with the Narragansett tribe in Rhode Island.

Right: The Pequods in Connecticut were provoked into war by the colonists in 1637, just after the first colony in Hartford had been established. They struck against isolated settlements and then waged a full-scale attack against the white settlers. Aided by neighboring Narragansetts and Mohegans, the colonists were able to virtually wipe out the Pequod tribe.

Above: The Wampanoag chief, Massasoit, is shown passing the peace pipe to John Carver, Governor of Plymouth in 1621. He stayed on friendly terms with the early colonists, but as time went on they began violating Indian territory. Warfare did not break out until after his sons, Metacomet and Wamsutta (called Philip and Alexander by the colonists), assumed joint leadership of the tribe.

Below: Some early American woodcuts idealized the Indians as genteel hunters. The two major roles of most Indian males were those of warrior and hunter. The bow and arrow was the chief weapon before the gun became available, and most hunting was done on foot, occasionally with the disguise of an animal skin.

week-long Ceremonial of Midwinter at the year's end, the sacred fire from the old year was destroyed and replaced with a new one. It was an opportunity for individuals to recall the good signs that had appeared in their dreams during the year to provide guidance in the coming year. The Iroquois were famous for their False Face Society, named after the being "False Face" who healed the sick. Members of this group were summoned to perform rituals, wearing masks that had been furnished with healing powers. The cured individual was then obliged to join the society.

The Senecas made up the largest Iroquoian tribe and, like the Mohawks, were extremely warlike and aggressive in nature. The Iroquoian-speaking Hurons were enemies of the League of Iroquois. They lived in a small territory in southern Ontario and were culturally similar to their linguistic relatives except for one unusual, infrequent ceremony—the Feast of the Dead. Hurons were terrified of death, believing that it caused illness among the living. The Feast of the Dead was a very solemn occasion held to bury all bodies and cremate them in a communal burial pit. This was the time for consoling the ghosts of the dead and releasing the souls to the distant world.

Although the Algonquian tribes were spread far and wide across the Northeast, they were considerably less powerful than the Iroquois. They were friendly and traded among themselves, but they were not united. In the far northeast Penobscot and Abnaki tribes lived a semi-nomadic life, contending with rough terrain and a hard

Above: Raids on white settlements were common, motivated by a natural Indian aggressiveness and the opportunity for material gain.

Right: Pontiac (*c.* 1715–1769), eloquent spokesman and Chief of the Ottawas, was an ally of the English but soon became disenchanted.

climate, always in the search for moose, their main source of food and clothing. In the south the Delaware Indians were typical of the Algonquian tribes that relied on farming for subsistence. Also known as Lenni-Lenape ("the people"), the Delawares were a loose federation of small villages. The men were the hunters, fishermen, warriors and healers. The women were the farmers, cooks and seamstresses, responsible for rearing children. The Delaware village was a haphazard arrangement around a central Big House. Living quarters were either rectangular buildings or wigwams, and each village included a sweathouse for steam baths, the remedy for disease and melancholy. After cleansing themselves, men repainted their bodies and women their faces with red (their favorite color), white and yellow dye. Red was usually associated with war because most Indians painted themselves before going into battle.

Children were given a great deal of independence as they grew up, and although premarital sexual activity was common, early marriages were rare. The marriage event was casual; the couple simply set up a wigwam together. Divorce was equally informal; the couple parted and the woman kept the house and children. Blood ties through the mother decided the succession of tribal chiefs. The Delaware Indians were very democratic and preferred to solve problems with reason rather than force. War was undertaken only on the decision of the council of old and wise men. Old age was treated with honor, and when an Indian died the body was placed in a shallow grave to allow

Above: Pontiac led a rebellion against the English at Detroit in 1763, at the end of the French and Indian War, but this adventure ended in failure.

Thayendanegea (Joseph Brant) of the Mohawks (1742–1807)

We have crossed the great lake and come to this kingdom with our superintendent, Colonel Johnson, from our Confederacy of the Six Nations and their allies, that we might see our father, the great king, and join in informing him, his counselors, and wise men, of the good intentions of the Indians, our brothers, and of their attachment to his majesty and his government.

Brother, the disturbances in America give great trouble to all our nations, and many strange stories have been told to us by the people of that country. The Six Nations, who always loved the king, sent a number of their chiefs and warriors with their superintendent to Canada last summer, where they engaged their allies to join with them in the defense of that country, and when it was invaded by the New England people they alone defeated them.

Brother, in that engagement we had several of our best warriors killed and wounded, and the Indians think it very hard they should have been so deceived by the white people in that country; many returning in great numbers, and no white people supporting the Indians, they were obliged to return to their villages and sit still. We now, brother, hope to see these bad children chastised, and that we may be enabled to tell the Indians who have always been faithful and ready to assist the king what his majesty intends.

Brother, the Mohawks, our particular nation, have on all occasions shown their zeal and loyalty to the great king; yet they have been very badly treated by the people in that country, the city of Albany laying an unjust claim to the lands on which our lower castle is built, as one Klock, and others do to those of Canajoharie, our upper village. We have often been assured by our late great friend, Sir William Johnson, who never deceived us, and we know he was told so, that the king and wise men here would do us justice. But this, notwithstanding all our applications, has never been done, and it makes us very uneasy. We also feel for the distress in which our brothers on the Susquehanna are likely to be involved by a mistake made in the boundary we settled in 1768. This also our superintendent has laid before the king. We have only, therefore, to request that his majesty will attend to this matter: it troubles our nation and they can not sleep easy in their beds. Indeed, it is very hard, when we have let the king's subjects have so much land for so little value, they should want to cheat us in this manner of the small spots we have left for our women and children to live on. We are tired out in making complaints and getting no redress. We therefore hope that the assurances now given us by the superintendent may take place and that he may have it in his power to procure us justice.

We shall truly report all that we hear from you to the Six Nations on our return. We are well informed there have been many Indians in this country who came without any authority from their own and gave us much trouble. We desire to tell you, brother, that this is not our case. We are warriors known to all the Nations, and are now here by approbation of many of them, whose sentiments we speak.

Brother, we hope that these things will be considered and that the king or his great men will give us such answer as will make our hearts light and glad before we go, and strengthen our hands, so that we may join our superintendent, Colonel Johnson, in giving satisfaction to all our Nations when we report to them on our return; for which purpose we hope soon to be accommodated with the passage.

To Lord George Germaine in London (1776)

Left: Indian raids on New England villages were frequent. Characteristically Indians surprised their victims at night in a quick attack and then made a hasty retreat.

Above: Thayendanegea, also known as Joseph Brant, was a Mohawk chief and leader of the Six Nations. He was educated in England and he, too, allied his forces with the British. Brant went to London in 1775–1776 to be sure that a British alliance would safeguard Indian land rights. Boswell interviewed him. Romney painted him. He made an impression on all who met him.

Tecumseh, Chief of the Shawnee (1768–1813)

It is true I am a Shawnee. My forefathers were warriors. Their son is a warrior. From them I take only my existence; from my tribe I take nothing. I am the maker of my own fortune; and oh! that I could make that of my red people, and of my country, as great as the conceptions of my mind, when I think of the Spirit that rules the universe. I would not then come to Governor Harrison to ask him to tear the treaty and to obliterate the landmark; but I would say to him: "Sir, you have liberty to return to your own country."

The being within, communing with past ages, tells me that once, nor until lately, there was no white man on this continent; that it then all belonged to red men, children of the same parents, placed on it by the Great Spirit that made them, to keep it, to traverse it, to enjoy its productions, and to fill it with the same race, once a happy race, since made miserable by the white people, who are never contented but always encroaching. The way, and the only way, to check and to stop this evil, is for all the red men to unite in claiming a common and equal right in the land, as it was at first, and should be yet; for it never was divided, but belongs to all for the use of each. For no part has a right to sell, even to each other, much less to strangers—those who want all, and will not do with less.

The white people have no right to take the land from the Indians, because they had it first; it is theirs. They may sell, but all must join. Any sale not made by all is not valid. The late sale is bad. It was made by a part only. Part do not know how to sell. It requires all to make a bargain for all. All red men have equal rights to the unoccupied land. The right of occupancy is as good in one place as in another. There can not be two occupations in the same place. The first excludes all others. It is not so in hunting or traveling; for there the same ground will serve many, as they may follow each other all day; but the camp is stationary, and that is occupancy. It belongs to the first who sits down on his blanket or skins which he has thrown upon the ground; and till he leaves it no other has a right.

To Governor Harrison at Vincennes, Indiana (1810)

Father, listen to your children! you have them now all before you. The war before this, our British father gave the hatchet to his red children when old chiefs were alive. They are now dead. In that war our father was thrown on his back by the Americans, and our father took them by the hand without our knowledge; and we are afraid that our father will do so again at this time.

Summer before last, when I came forward with my red brethren and was ready to take up the hatchet in favor of our British father, we were told not to be in a hurry; that he had not yet determined to fight the Americans.

Listen! When war was declared, our father stood up and gave us the tomahawk, and told us that he was ready to strike the Americans; that he wanted our assistance, and that he would certainly get us our lands back, which the Americans had taken from us.

Listen! You told us at that time to bring forward our families to this place, and we did so; and you promised to take care of them, and that they should want for nothing while the men would go and fight the enemy. That we need not trouble ourselves about the enemy's

Above: Shawnee chief Tecumseh traveled extensively throughout the Northeast and Southeast in a valiant effort to unite all tribes against increasing white settlement, but he realized only partial success. In 1810 he met with Governor William Henry Harrison of Indiana to air his grievances against the English. Harrison drew his sword in anger but quickly withdrew. Tecumseh was defeated at Tippecanoe the next year.

the soul an easy departure to the realm where there was no suffering.

Algonquians who lived in the most western reaches of the Northeast, around the Great Lakes, relied heavily on a diet of wild rice. Tobacco, a key crop, was accepted as a gift from the spirits and was used during rituals and for socializing. Maple sugar was also valuable. Seminomadic tribes returned to their villages in the summer to plant their crops. This was also the time of year for religious festivals honoring Manitou, the highest ranking god. Summer was the season for war, for small-scale raids. Young men were not permitted to go to war or to hunt until they had undertaken the Vision Quest. As in other tribes, this was the period of solitary fasting in the woods, waiting to receive the guardian spirit. The Midewiwin was a secret curing society peculiar to western Algonquians. Its members were responsible for performing the Grand Medicine Dance. They danced themselves into a frenzy, throwing magic shells that cured ills when they touched the diseased body.

The Menominees were a seminomadic tribe of the same area that depended on wild rice for food. They were skilled weavers who produced unusual woven bags made of vegetable fibers and buffalo hair. The Winnebagos in Wisconsin were the friends and allies of the Menominees and had the same customs. The main difference was that their villages were arranged according to two moieties and the clans

garrisons; that we knew nothing about them, and that our father would attend to that part of the business. You also told your red children that you would take good care of your garrison here, which made our hearts glad.

Listen! When we were last at the Rapids, it is true we gave you little assistance. It is hard to fight people who live like ground-hogs.

Father, listen! Our fleet has gone out; we know they have fought; we have heard the great guns, but know nothing of what has happened to our father with one arm. Our ships have gone one way, and we are much astonished to see our father tying up everything and preparing to run away the other, without letting his red children know what his intentions are. You always told us to remain here and take care of our lands. It made our hearts glad to hear that was your wish. Our great father, the king, is the head, and you represent him. You always told us that you would never draw your foot off British ground; but now, father, we see you are drawing back, and we are sorry to see our father doing so without seeing the enemy. We must compare our father's conduct to a fat animal that carries its tail upon its back, but when affrighted it drops it between its legs and runs off.

Listen, father! The Americans have not yet defeated us by land; neither are we sure that they have done so by water; we therefore wish to remain here and fight our enemy should they make their appearance. If they defeat us, we will then retreat with our father.

At the Battle of the Rapids, last war, the Americans certainly defeated us; and when we retreated to our father's fort in that place the gates were shut against us. We were afraid it would now be the case, but instead of that we now see our British father preparing to march out of his garrison.

Father! You have got the arms and ammunition which our great father sent for his red children. If you have an idea of going away, give them to us, and you may go and welcome; for us, our lives are in the hands of the Great Spirit. We are determined to defend our lands, and if it is His will we wish to leave our bones upon them.

To General Henry A Proctor (1813)

that made up the moieties. Marriage partners were required to be from the opposite moiety. Kinship was based on cross relationships, and it was especially important for a boy to seek guidance from a cross-related male.

Sauks and Foxes were the Winnebago's enemies. They were fierce warriors who placed great value on bravery in battle. The greatest act of courage was to touch the enemy war leader during battle, and for his success the warrior received a new name. Victory in battle was celebrated with a scalp dance around the fire, at which time warriors recounted their feats in gory detail.

The eastern territories were the first of North America to experience full-scale encroachment by the Europeans and the first to suffer the effects of white settlement. The Spanish had established a foothold in St Augustine, Florida as early as 1565, and were followed by Dutch and French traders. Under the leadership of Samuel de Champlain, the French settled in Quebec, Canada in 1603. La Salle brought a second group over in 1663. After many difficult years he eventually reached the mouth of the Mississippi River, erecting forts along the way, and he installed a permanent settlement in Louisiana. In the meantime the Dutch settled in the Delaware Valley in 1618.

The first Europeans did not pose an immediate threat to the woodland Indians. They were friendly traders who brought valuable supplies, such as guns from Holland, and as a consequence developed mutually beneficial relationships with the natives. The French established valuable trade links with the Hurons and remained their strong ally in war. They even trained their own warriors in Indian camps. It was the Europeans who came to North America for the sole purpose of colonizing who caused the greatest harm, the first of which were the English. In 1607 a shipload of men had reached Jamestown, Virginia and established a settlement that began to grow slowly. In 1620 the Pilgrims landed at Plymouth Bay in Massachusetts and one year later they celebrated the first Thanksgiving with the Indians who had helped them through the first terrible winter. Once they had survived the initial hardships with the help of the Indian, they considered him an impediment. Indian values clashed too much with European values, and colonists saw no hope of converting them to their form of civilization. As settlements prospered and expanded, white settlers appropriated more land. The influx of Europeans upset the natural balance of Indian life and brought with it the perils of disease and alcohol. Strange new diseases coursed along the coast and wiped out large numbers of Indians even before warfare was able to take its toll. As settlers laid claim to more land, local conflicts became commonplace as Indians strove to protect their territory.

Ultimately the Indian population, except for the Iroquois, was too small, powerless and disunified to mount a mean-

Above: Any white man was a likely target for Indian warriors. Some tribes were particularly renowned for their savage treatment of victims. In some, cases, however, captives were adopted into the tribe.

ingful retaliation. Compared to the Europeans, Indians were unsophisticated in the art of warfare. They fought with simple weapons until the advent of guns. Even the iron tomahawk, the trademark of the Algonquians, was forged by the early settlers. Throughout the 1600s Indians caused considerable damage and loss of life, but they suffered even more. As early as 1622 Powhatan resorted to war against the Virginia settlers when they seized more Indian land to grow tobacco, and he suffered defeat. King Philip (Metacomet) organized the Wampanoags and Narragansetts, the Indians who had been responsible for helping the early colonists survive, in Rhode Island against the English and their Mohegan allies in 1674. He felt that Indian survival could be achieved only by driving out the English, and after two years of fighting and causing hundreds of deaths, he was soundly defeated. The Delaware tribes formed their own federation as a protection against the settlers soon after their arrival, but they were overwhelmed by sheer numbers in a short period of time. They were powerless against their western neighbors, the mighty Iroquois, who seized nearby Indian territory for hunting grounds, and by 1690 many had begun migrating west, some joining the Huron tribe. The first Indian reservation, established in 1758 by the Brainerd brothers, was not a success and the Delawares continued their westward move to avoid harassment by settlers, abandoning what little land they had left.

Above: Dan Waupoose, a Menominee chief, was photographed in 1943 in his feathered headdress. The warbonnet was a creation of eastern Indians and was a testament of a warrior's achievements and courage in battle.

Next page: Students in a physics class at the Carlisle Indian School, Pennsylvania, founded in 1879. Nine years earlier the United States had begun its program to fund Indian education, and children were forced to attend missionary or government-run schools.

During the 1700s the woodland Indians found it more advantageous and rewarding to ally themselves with the Europeans, but the end result was that they fought each other. In 1763, after eight years of warring, the English and their Iroquois allies were the triumphant victors over the French and their allies in the bid for more territory. The Iroquois were at the peak of their power. At the beginning of the century they had control of the fur trade in the Northeast, having vanquished neighboring tribes in the effort, and when the Tuscarora became the Sixth Nation in 1722, the Iroquois were the undisputed Indian authority in the region.

In 1776 the colonists rose up against the British and their Indian allies in the fight for independence. Under the leadership of General George Washington, the colonists achieved their goal. The loyalties of the various Iroquois tribes were divided and the power of the Iroquois crumbled. The League disintegrated, the tribes split up, and many moved into Canada, where a strong settlement was able to survive and maintain its cultural heritage. A further result

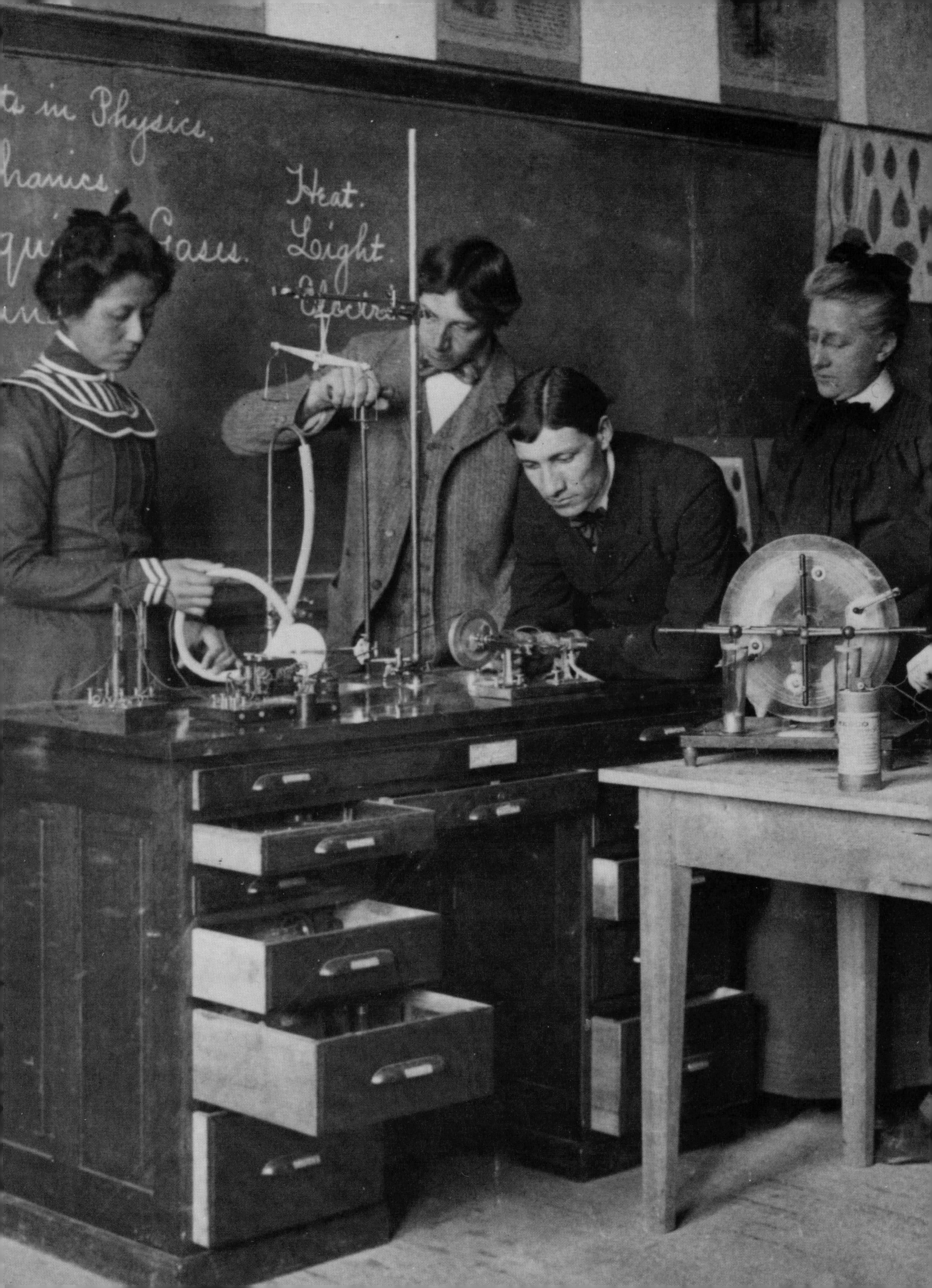
ts in Physics.
hanics.
Gases.
Heat.
Light

Left: An 1847 daguerreotype of Watchful Fox, a Sauk Indian born around 1780. The Algonquian-speaking Sauks lived on the western shore of Lake Michigan, where they were buffalo hunters and farmers.

Above: Jesse Cornplanter, descendant of Cornplanter, the famous Seneca chief, carves out a ceremonial mask like the one shown on the following page.

of the American Revolution was the opening of the West for settlement. The earlier British proclamation forbidding settlement by whites beyond the Appalachians had been ignored. Colonies were expanding continuously, driving the Indian population into a position of a minority.

Traders and trappers were the first to venture into the Great Northwest. As settlers followed, Indians were pushed even farther west. The Indian Removal Act in 1830, the handiwork of Andrew Jackson, forced the Indians to move west of the Mississippi. In spite of a few humane efforts to help the Indian, these native peoples found themselves on the brink of their worst period in history. The Sauks and Foxes had ceded their territory to the US government at the beginning of the century and moved onto the plains. When their chief,,Black Hawk, returned east in 1832 to renegotiate the agreement, his party was attacked. After

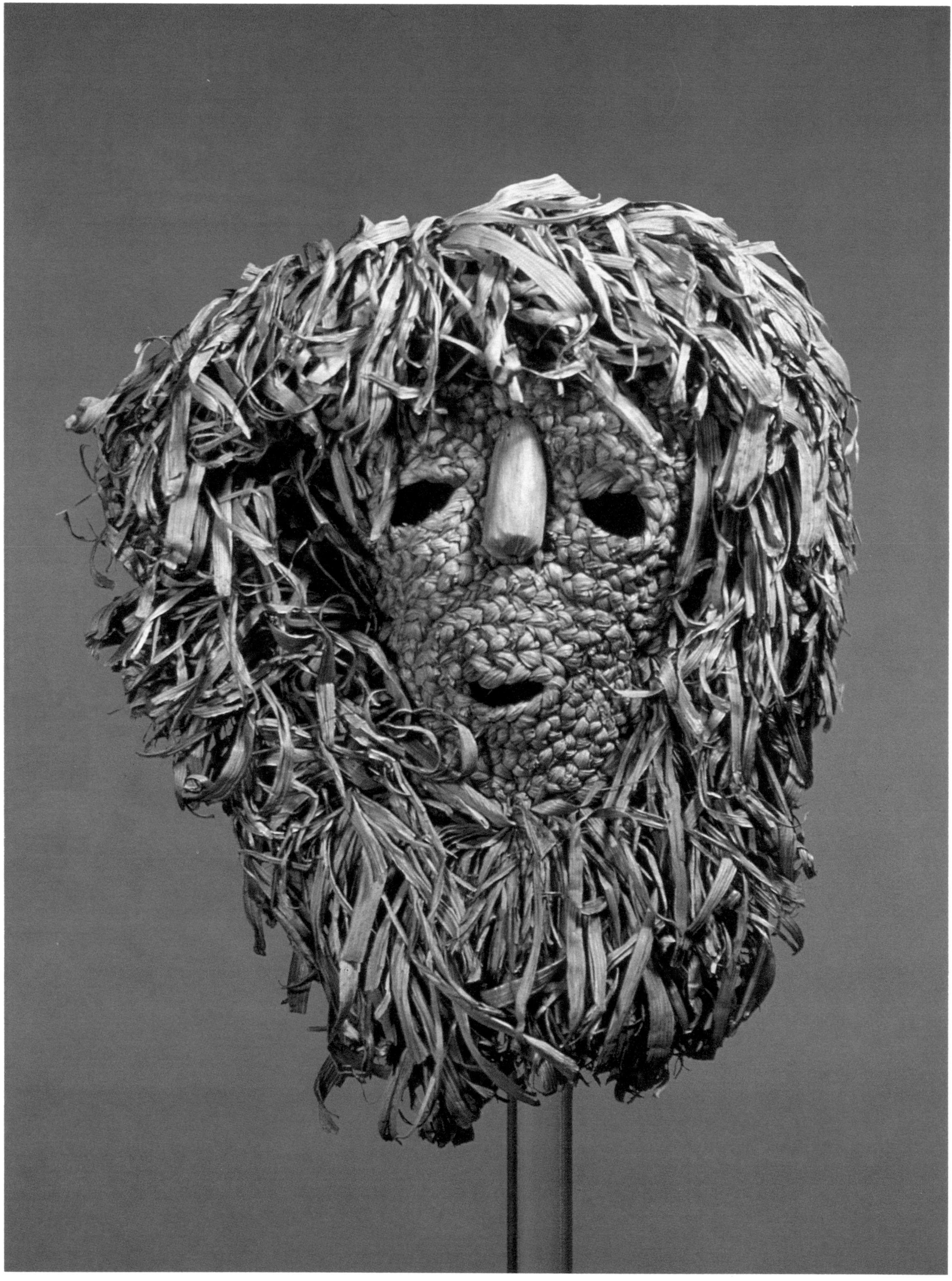

Above: A modern Seneca corn husk mask. Members of the Husk Face Society, a small religious group, wore these masks and danced during the Midwinter Ceremonial when they prophesied plentiful crops. The mask is made almost entirely of corn husks, braided and sewn together. The nose is wood or husk. To many Indian tribes, corn was the most important crop, and many ceremonies were felt to be necessary to ensure a proper harvest.

Red Jacket on the Religion of the White Man and the Red (1805)

Friend and Brother: It was the will of the Great Spirit that we should meet together this day. He orders all things and has given us a fine day for our council. He has taken His garment from before the sun and caused it to shine with brightness upon us. Our eyes are opened that we see clearly; our ears are unstopped that we have been able to hear distinctly the words you have spoken. For all these favors we thank the Great Spirit, and Him only.

Brother, this council fire was kindled by you. It was at your request that we came together at this time. We have listened with attention to what you have said. You requested us to speak our minds freely. This gives us great joy; for we now consider that we stand upright before you and can speak what we think. All have heard your voice and all speak to you now as one man. Our minds are agreed.

Brother, you say you want an answer to your talk before you leave this place. It is right you should have one, as you are a great distance from home and we do not wish to detain you. But first we will look back a little and tell you what our fathers have told us and what we have heard from the white people.

Brother, listen to what we say. There was a time when our forefathers owned this great island. Their seats extended from the rising to the setting sun. The Great Spirit had made it for the use of Indians. He had created the buffalo, the deer, and other animals for food. He had made the bear and the beaver. Their skins served us for clothing. He had scattered them over the country and taught us how to take them. He had caused the earth to produce corn for bread. All this He had done for His red children because He loved them. If we had some disputes about our hunting-ground they were generally settled without the shedding of much blood.

But an evil day came upon us. Your forefathers crossed the great water and landed on this island. Their numbers were small. They found friends and not enemies. They told us they had fled from their own country for fear of wicked men and had come here to enjoy their religion. They asked for a small seat. We took pity on them, granted their request, and they sat down among us. We gave them corn and meat; they gave us poison in return.

The white people, brother, had now found our country. Tidings were carried back and more came among us. Yet we did not fear them. We took them to be friends. They called us brothers. We believed them and gave them a larger seat. At length their numbers had greatly increased. They wanted more land; they wanted our country. Our eyes were opened and our minds became uneasy. Wars took place. Indians were hired to fight against Indians, and many of our people were destroyed. They also brought strong liquor among us. It was strong and powerful, and has slain thousands.

Brother, our seats were once large and yours were small. You have now become a great people, and we have scarcely a place left to spread our blankets. You have got our country, but are not satisfied; you want to force your religion upon us.

Brother, continue to listen. You say that you are sent to instruct us how to worship the Great Spirit agreeably to His mind; and, if we do not take hold of the religion which you white people teach we shall be unhappy hereafter. You say that you are right and we are lost. How do we know this to be true? We understand that your religion is written in a Book. If it was intended for us, as well as you, why has not the Great Spirit given to us, and not only to us, but why did He not give to our forefathers the knowledge of that Book, with the means of understanding it rightly. We only know what you tell us about it. How shall we know when to believe, being so often deceived by the white people?

Brother, you say there is but one way to worship and serve the Great Spirit. If there is but one religion, why do you white people differ so much about it? Why not all agreed, as you can all read the Book?

Brother, we do not understand these things. We are told that your religion was given to your forefathers and has been handed down from father to son. We also have a religion which was given to our forefathers and has been handed down to us, their children. We worship in that way. It teaches us to be thankful for all the favors we receive, to love each other, and to be united. We never quarrel about religion.

Brother, the Great Spirit has made us all, but He has made a great difference between His white and His red children. He has given us different complexions and different customs. To you He has given the arts. To these He has not opened our eyes. We know these things to be true. Since He has made so great a difference between us in other things, why may we not conclude that He has given us a different religion according to our understanding? The Great Spirit does right. He knows what is best for His children; we are satisfied.

Brother, we do not wish to destroy your religion or take it from you. We only want to enjoy our own.

Brother, you say you have not come to get our land or our money, but to enlighten our minds. I will now tell you that I have been at your meetings and saw you collect money from the meeting. I can not tell what this money was intended for, but suppose that it was for your minister; and, if we should conform to your way of thinking, perhaps you may want some from us.

Brother, we are told that you have been preaching to the white people in this place. These people are our neighbors. We are acquainted with them. We will wait a little while and see what effect your preaching has upon them. If we find it does them good, makes them honest, and less disposed to cheat Indians, we will then consider again of what you have said.

Brother, you have now heard our answer to your talk, and this is all we have to say at present. As we are going to part, we will come and take you by the hand, and hope the Great Spirit will protect you on your journey and return you safe to your friends.

Left: The shaman was a key figure in every tribe of North American Indians, but his or her function was distinct and varied from tribe to tribe. Leslie Gray, shown here, is a Native American of Oneida Iroquois descent and is a contemporary shaman who is reviving the technique of problem solving that was characteristic of the indigenous people of North America. She is a psychologist who incorporates ancient shamanic practices into contemporary work. Beating the drum is a ritual technique that is used to encourage visions. The monotonous and repetitious sounds produce a "sonic driving" through which one's state of consciousness is altered, thereby enhancing problem-solving capabilities. Ancient shamans resolved problems by guiding themselves or others through a visionary experience.

three months of fighting, Black Hawk retreated to Iowa, only to be pursued by the military and massacred as he tried to surrender. The US government had succeeded in ridding the Northeast of domination by the Indians. The few tribes that had not already left were expelled to Indian Territory to the west, with few exceptions. All of this had taken place by 1867, and by then the Mississippi Valley was brimming with new settlers.

The following century saw a variety of inconsistent government policies and a new Indian emergence. In 1887 the General Allotment Act was passed to break up Indian property into individual parcels, in the hope that Indians would farm or graze it. That did not happen and in the end many Indians simply sold off or leased their property to whites. Other efforts to assimilate Indians by educating children on government-run schools failed miserably. In 1934 the Indian Reorganization Act made all Indians born on US soil American citizens; they were no longer restricted to reservations and they were allowed to vote. In compensation for earlier failures, the federal government provided a range of services and funds to help the Indian and also tried to encourage self-government. After World War II many of the thousands of Indians who left the reservations to serve in the war effort experienced a profound culture shock when they tried to return to their old lifestyle.

A new Indian activism was born, and out of this the all-Indian National Congress of American Indians was established to look after Indian interests. This new breed of Indian was responsible for creating the Indian Claims Commission in 1946 to encourage Indians to reclaim old tribal land from the US. The federal government, however, began to swing in the other direction, ending much of its aid and once again trying to force absorption into mainstream white society. This, too, failed. In response the government allocated funds and encouraged Indians to handle their own affairs independently. In 1961 the Commissioner of Indian Affairs post was created to provide the Indians with a spokesperson in Washington. A fresh aggressiveness in the last 20 years resulted in confrontations and court claims in the mid-1970s. The Wampanoags successfully reclaimed property in Massachusetts and the Penobscot and Passamaquoddy in Maine are now claiming extensive land rights as well as a financial compensation. These proceedings have caused confusion, financial concern and conflict within state governments; in their wake Indians in Connecticut, Rhode Island and New York and in the Midwest and West are making land claims and demanding a variety of commercial rights. A simultaneous cultural renewal has evolved as Indians struggle to retain their identity. For the first time since the early 1600s the general prosperity of Native Americans has finally begun to progress. The American Indian has not died out and as recent history seems to indicate, will continue to have a place in North America.

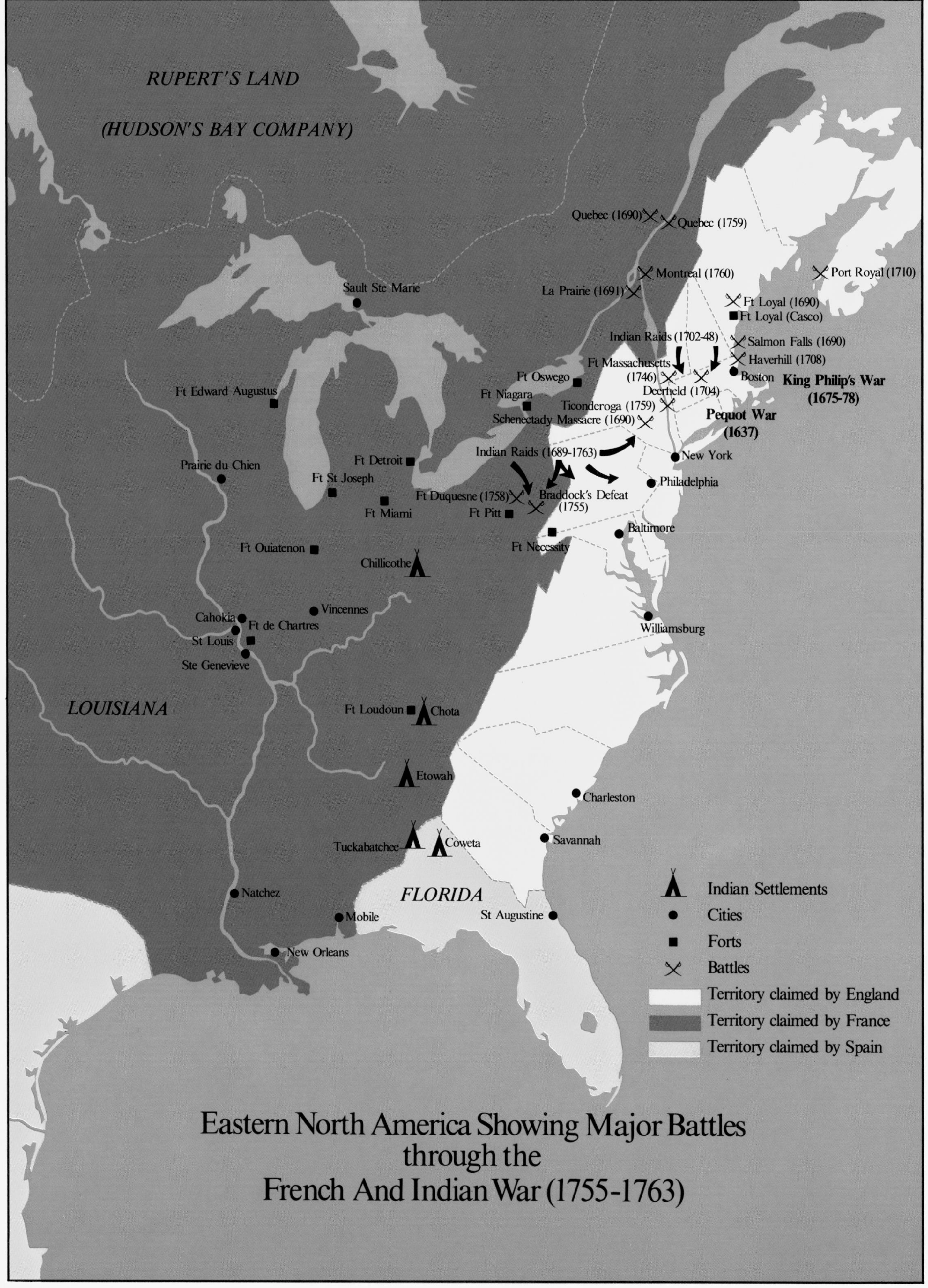

RUPERT'S LAND
(HUDSON'S BAY COMPANY)
Quebec (1690)
Quebec (1759)
Montreal (1760)
Port Royal (1710)
La Prairie (1691)
Ft Loyal (1690)
Ft Loyal (Casco)
Sault Ste Marie
Indian Raids (1702-48)
Salmon Falls (1690)
Haverhill (1708)
Ft Massachusetts (1746)
Boston
King Philip's War (1675-78)
Ft Oswego
Deerfield (1704)
Ft Edward Augustus
Ft Niagara
Ticonderoga (1759)
Pequot War (1637)
Schenectady Massacre (1690)
Indian Raids (1689-1763)
New York
Ft Detroit
Prairie du Chien
Ft St Joseph
Philadelphia
Ft Duquesne (1758)
Braddock's Defeat (1755)
Ft Miami
Ft Pitt
Baltimore
Ft Ouiatenon
Ft Necessity
Chillicothe
Vincennes
Cahokia
Ft de Chartres
Williamsburg
St Louis
Ste Genevieve
LOUISIANA
Ft Loudoun
Chota
Etowah
Charleston
Tuckabatchee
Coweta
Savannah
Natchez
FLORIDA
Mobile
St Augustine
New Orleans
Indian Settlements
Cities
Forts
Battles
Territory claimed by England
Territory claimed by France
Territory claimed by Spain

Eastern North America Showing Major Battles through the French And Indian War (1755-1763)

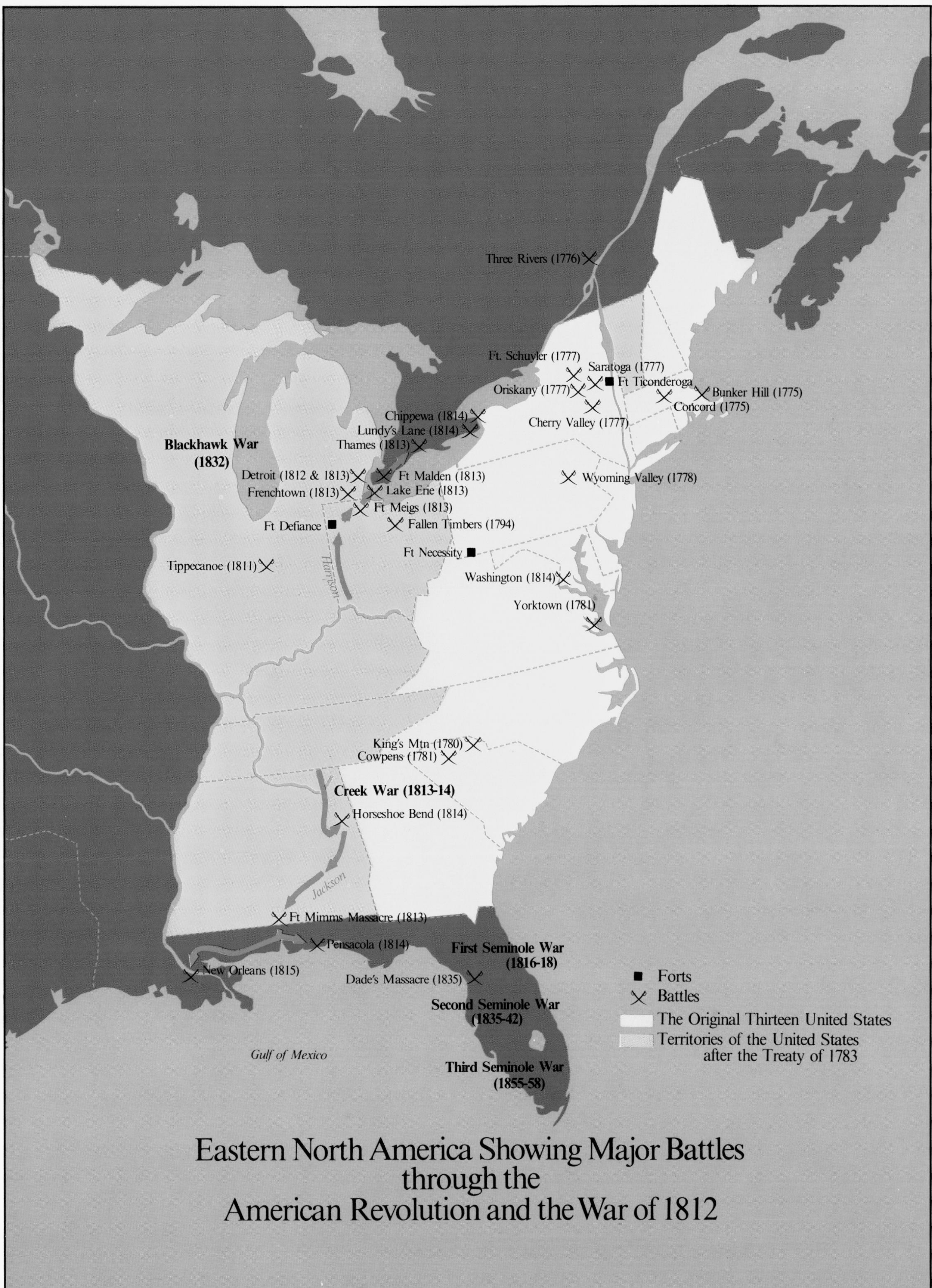

Eastern North America Showing Major Battles through the American Revolution and the War of 1812

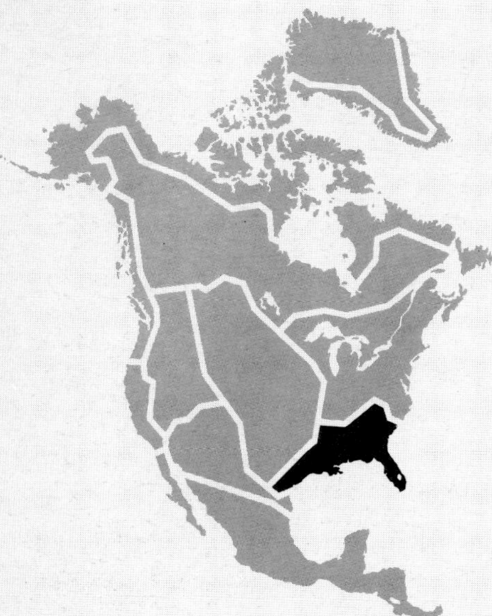

INDIANS OF THE SOUTHEAST

Below: A Choctaw man in Louisiana, *circa* 1909 demonstrates how to shoot a poison dart through a cane blowgun. This weapon was unique to Southeastern Indians and was used to hunt squirrels, rabbits and birds.

Right: A young Seminole girl, with her hair wrapped characteristically around a hoop, sews at the Glades County Reservation School in Florida. The Seminoles developed a style of brightly colored fabric patchwork that was incorporated into clothing for men and women. With the use of the sewing machine they were able to devise more intricate patterns.

The territory from the Atlantic coast to the western Mississippi Valley and from the Gulf of Mexico to Virginia and Kentucky in the north was the home of a large array of tribes that spoke many languages but were similar by virtue of their lifestyle. Indians in the Southeast all lived in villages and were primarily agriculturalists. They were blessed with a mild climate, ample rainfall, lush and fertile land abundant in animal life, and rivers and coastal waters full of fish.

Prior to the arrival of the white man, the Indian population in the Southeast consisted of somewhere between 150 and 200 diverse tribes, each with its own language and dialects. The Iroquoian-speaking Cherokee and Tuscarora lived in the northern ranges and were the most numerous

SINGER

Indian Tribes of the Southeast

Alibamu
Apalachee
Atakapa
Biloxi
Calusa
Catawba
Chatot
Cherokee
Chickasaw
Chitimacha
Choctaw
Creek
Croatan
Koasati
Kusa
Lower Creek
Lumbee
Muskogean
Natchez
Seminole
Shawnee
Taensa
Timucua (Timuquanan)
Tunica
Tuscarora
Tutelo
Upper Creek
Yamasee
Yuchi

Above: A Cherokee elder heats a stone axehead over a fire at the Cherokee reservation in North Carolina.

Left: Artist Frederick Kemmelmeyer painted Christopher Columbus and his party landing on San Salvador, now called Watling's Island, in the West Indies. Taino Indians look on. The Spanish conquistadores were the first Europeans to encounter Indians on North American soil, and they came in search of precious trade goods and to take slaves. In a short time they became known for their cruel treatment of the Indians.

Indians of the region. The Muskogean-speaking Choctaw, Chickasaw and Creeks were the dominant tribes farther south when the first Europeans arrived, by which time all of the Southeast cultures had reached their cultural peak of development. In general, they were accomplished craftsmen—good potters, basket weavers and builders, and proficient at working in stone. Women cultivated crops of corn, millet, squash, beans, melons and tobacco while men hunted turkey, bear, deer and opossum. After a ritual prayer, men departed for the hunt individually or in small bands, attracting their prey by imitating their call or by disguising themselves in animal skins. The kill was accomplished with a bow and arrow or by shooting darts through a cane blowgun. Some tribes, like the Seminoles, relied heavily on a diet of fish, which they caught with poles and hooks, spears, nets or poison darts. These Indians also supplemented their diet with nuts, berries, and other foraged vegetables. Indians had a great deal of respect for natural resources and, because they believed that all supplies were ultimately limited, they prayed for replenishment. Thus, when the early Europeans arrived, they found a race of peoples that seemed at one with the land and that had caused very little disruption to the environment.

Ponce de Leon was the first of a line of Spanish conquistadores to attempt to conquer North America. He first landed in Florida in 1513 and returned in 1521, intending to conquer and colonize. The Indians had received him on friendly terms during his first visit, but in the interim they suffered from the brutality of other Spanish slave raiders. By the time Ponce de Leon returned in 1521, the Indians had turned against the Spanish and they wounded him on his arrival.

Tribes of the Northeast and the Southeast were the most highly organized north of Mexico, and many were united in strong confederacies. The Creeks organized themselves into a federation of intertribal councils comprised of representatives from each community. The Southeastern tribes were organized according to the clan system, with chiefdom and kinship based on descent from the mother. Although women were highly regarded, men were the decision makers, and all business that affected the community was handled by councils of men. In the Creek tribe the town councils met every day to discuss tribal affairs. Clan loyalty was of utmost importance and revenge for crimes committed against a clan member was taken seriously. It was usually the reason for going to war.

Creek towns were laid out around a public square consisting of summer and winter council meeting buildings, a hot house for winter activities and a chunkey yard in one corner for sports and games. Houses were arranged in small groups around the square, with the modest houses of the poorer families concentrated on the fringes of the village. The summer council meeting building was built with open sides and the winter one with walls. They were rectangular buildings, with log frames and walls plastered with mud and grass. In the middle of the bark roof a hole was left to allow for smoke to escape, since the sacred fires were kept burning all the time. Because the rooms were very warm, clothing was minimal and simple. In the warmer parts of the Southeast houses were also built with one or more sides

In 1519 the Spaniards made their way into Mexico to begin their violent conquest of Mesoamerica under the leadership of Hernando Cortez. He captured Tenochtitlan, the Aztec capital, and seized its king, Montezuma.

left open. Each house was occupied by several families of a single clan. Usually villages were surrounded by a palisade, or protective wall, of plastered staked fences interrupted periodically by tall watchtowers.

The Cherokee village was centered around a huge seven-sided Town House that was dome shaped and made of earth. It was large enough to hold crowds of 500 for ceremonies and council meetings. Surrounding it were the games field and community farming land. On the edges of those fields were the houses. They were small, rectangular buildings covered with clay and roofed with bark.

For the Indians of the region warfare was as important an activity as hunting. It was therefore frequent but usually on a small scale. In addition to settling disputes with nearby tribes, it was also the means by which warriors established their reputations. Boys were not regarded as men until they had proved their skill and courage in battle, and the status of the male in the community was based on his achievements in war. War was also a sporting activity, and Indians traveled far and wide when necessary in search of it. Before engaging in war, a council of wise men convened with the chief to deliberate. If they decided to go to war, a force of young male volunteers was organized for battle. The preparation for battle was surrounded by ritual, including fasting, feasting and body painting, all of which took several days to complete. Indians relied on stealth and surprise for their success. They were also very superstitious and would retreat immediately if they were detected by the enemy

Left: George Catlin (1796–1872) painted this portrait of Osceola, the handsome young Creek warrior and able leader of the Seminoles shortly before the Indian's death in 1838. The Indians in Florida had enjoyed good relations with the Spanish, but not with the colonists.

From 1816 to 1818 they were engaged in the First Seminole War with Andrew Jackson, who was gathering runaway slaves and provoking the Indians in the process. In 1830 he passed the Indian Removal Act and the effort to rid the Southeast of Indians was well underway. The Seminoles were pressured into signing the Treaty of Payne's Landing in 1832, thereby selling their territory and agreeing to move west to Indian Territory within three years.

Osceola assumed the leadership of the Seminoles in their bitter struggle to keep possession of their homes. Those Indians who didn't move west retreated deeper into the swamplands. In a meeting with government officials, Osceola impetuously slashed the treaty with his knife as a gesture of his displeasure. After a day of imprisonment, he signed the treaty only to disappear with his forces into the swamps, where he organized guerrilla attacks against the white settlers.

This marked the beginning of the Second Seminole War, which lasted until 1842. In 1835 Osceola murdered an Indian agent, Wiley Thompson, in revenge for his earlier imprisonment. In 1837 he was tricked into a truce, seized and thrown into prison in Fort Moultrie, South Carolina. He died there three months later, all the while harboring great bitterness against the white settlers. After considerable loss of life on both sides, most of the weary Seminoles were rounded up and herded to Indian Territory. Some remained in the Everglades, where they fought a Third Seminole War in 1855 and were again defeated. A small number remained in the state of Florida, proud that they never relinquished their homes.

Below: The Spaniards were notorious for the barbaric and ferocious way they dealt with the Indians. Bartolome de las Casas was a Spanish Dominican friar who remained the loyal friend of the Indians in the Southeast and was determined to help them. In addition to a history of the Indians, he wrote *New Laws* that was adopted to protect the Indians from mistreatment. He wrote extensive and detailed descriptions of the atrocious activities of the conquistadores, perhaps exaggerated, in a deliberate effort to promote the welfare of the Indian. The *Black Legend* of the English painted a similar unfavorable picture of the Spanish.

before the attack or if they encountered a bad omen. The victorious return from battle was celebrated by several more days of elaborate ceremonies.

The roles of men and women among Indians were clearly divided, and children were raised accordingly. The men went to war and hunted. They were also responsible for clearing the fields, which the women then cultivated and harvested. Women were responsible for raising the children and looking after the home, which included making pottery, weaving baskets, tanning animal skins, making clothing and cooking. Older women arranged the marriage matches, but the couple in question made the final decision. The young man was required to provide a home before the couple could live together, since marriage was the result of completing a year of cohabitation. If they wished to part at that time, they could easily do so. If they remained together, they were considered married. Marriage within the clan was forbidden. Polygamy was common in the Southeast, but only if the male could afford more than one wife and only if the first wife approved.

Indians in the Southeast were among the most permissive of American Indians, and these premarital sexual relationships were totally acceptable. Illegitimate children were raised by the mother's family, but among some tribes, they carried a stigma and were badly treated. After birth, the child was bound to a cradleboard, where it remained for the full first year of its life, with its head held down to flatten the skull. A flat skull was considered an attractive feature.

Most tribes in this region believed that their universe consisted of three separate worlds: the perfect Upper World, the unsettled Lower World and This World, the realm in the middle. In their daily life Indians strove to find a balance between the two extreme worlds and between good and bad forces. A large number of supernatural beings inhabited their universe, the most important of whom was the sun god, represented on earth as fire. The main, sacred fire in the village was kept burning all year long and was used to light the individual fires in each building. These were also kept burning throughout the year.

Complicated rituals accompanied the planting and harvesting of crops. The busk, or Green Corn Dance, was the most sacred holiday and took place when the corn ripened in the autumn, marking the end of the year. During the four- to eight-day ceremony, the sacred fire was destroyed and replaced with a new fire to symbolize the new year. Included in the ritual were fasting, feasting and bathing, as well as a thorough cleaning of all living areas. All crimes, except murder, that had been committed during the year were forgiven at this time.

In the South the Spanish conquistadores were the first Europeans to encounter the Indians, or Los Indios, so named by Christopher Columbus when he reached San Salvadore in 1493, thinking he had reached the East Indies. Inspired by the stories of gold Columbus had discovered in the Caribbean, Juan Ponce de Leon made his way west to Florida in 1513, with the intention of conquering and colonizing. Hernando de Soto followed in 1593, the first of the conquistadores to come for slaves, looting, plundering, and introducing new diseases at the same time. In 1565 the Spanish finally succeeded in establishing a permanent settlement in St Augustine for the purpose of spreading Christianity among the Indians.

Above: Micanopy, a Seminole chief, poses with his peace medal.

Right: Billy Bowlegs, a Mikasuki Seminole, assumed leadership of the Seminoles during the Second Seminole War after Osceola's capture by government forces in 1837.

Below: William Weatherford, a half-breed Creek, led a force of Creeks in the surprise attack on Fort Mims in Alabama and in the ensuing massacre, one of the many battles of the Creek War of 1813.

764

Left: This sixteenth-century figure of a cougar is a relic from an ancient Indian site at Key Marco (now Marco Island) off the west coast of Florida. At the end of the last century archeologist Frank Hamilton Cushing discovered by chance a large number of artifacts on this otherwise deserted island. The figure shown here is six inches tall and was carved with tools made of sharks' teeth. When the carving was completed it was covered with a protective greasy coating. Other carvings discovered include masks and numerous small animal figures, some of which were made with movable parts. The creators of these objects are unknown but are thought to be related to the Muskogeans. These skilled artisans made excellent use of the materials at hand, especially the large supply of shells washed up by the sea, which they turned into tools or used to decorate carvings.

Above: This cane basket is a product of the Chitimacha Indians who lived at the mouth of the Mississippi River. Basketmaking is one of the oldest of Indian crafts and one at which Indians all over North America excelled. A variety of materials, including reeds, roots, bark and grasses, were woven by plaiting, coiling or twining to produce an enormous assortment of shapes and designs. Decoration was applied by means of vegetable dye or by incorporating feathers, shells, beads, quills or buckskin. In the Southeast dried cane was usually used and it was woven by a technique called twilled plaiting. The warp and weft are identical in size and shape in plaited baskets, and the result was a very angular design characteristic of Southeastern basketry. Natural cane was either green or yellow. Black and red vegetable dyes from walnut and oak bark respectively completed the color range and were used for decoration.

Left: During World War II thousands of Indians joined the services. Lieutenant Woody J Cochran, a Cherokee from Oklahoma, was a bomber pilot decorated for distinguished service in 1943.

Right: Lieutenant Ernest Childers, a Creek, served in the US Army and was awarded the Congressional Medal of Honor in Italy in 1944.

Below: Delegates from 34 tribes pose in front of the Creek Council House in Indian Territory around 1880.

Left: A Florida Seminole spears a garfish from a dugout around 1930. This type of boat was carved out of a log.

Below left: Two twentieth-century Seminole women at the Seminole Indian Agency in Florida cook cane syrup.

Right: A Cherokee boy and girl pose in traditional deerskin garments at their reservation in North Carolina in 1939. In the South men generally went bare-chested and women wore a one-piece dress.

By the time the English began colonizing the territory to the north and the French had laid claim to the Mississippi Valley and Louisiana, the Southeastern Indians had already suffered considerably. Both the British and French quickly established strong trade ties with the southern Indians, eventually securing a hold over them by supplying goods on credit. By the middle of the 1700s the various tribes, and Creeks in particular, had adapted their lives to foreign goods such as guns, knives, cloth and whiskey and become dependent on the trade. The European demand for slaves encouraged their Indian allies to raid other Southeastern tribes to take captives for trade.

By 1763 the French had lost most of their eastern territory, and in that year the British banned all white settlement beyond the Appalachians. In spite of this, settlers pushed south and west. Disease spread rapidly among the Indians, decimating tribes. In 1738 one half of the Cherokee population had succumbed to a smallpox epidemic. The constant warfare, increased slave trade and strange diseases took their toll and depleted the strength and numbers of the Indian population. The Creek confederacy was divided during the Revolutionary War, and both the Creeks and Cherokees were badly beaten in the war after supporting the British. Valuable lands in the south were seized from the Indians when Eli Whitney's cotton gin boosted the cotton industry. As tribes dispersed, their cultural traditions began to weaken, they began to intermarry with whites and to convert to Christianity. Only the five main tribes remained—the Choctaw, Chickasaw, Creek, Seminole and Cherokee—and these tribes came to be known as the Five Civilized Tribes.

Then in 1785 the Cherokees made their first treaty with the US government, handing over all their land east of the Blue Ridge. In the late 1700s Alex McGillivray, the half-Scot, half-Creek leader of his tribe, was able to unify his people against the onslaught of white settlement. With his death in 1793 the Creeks crumbled into disarray again. In response to the general disorder among Indians, the great Shawnee chief Tecumseh traveled up the coast into the Northeast and over to the Great Lakes in a valiant effort to consolidate all Indians, restore customs and reclaim their rightful land. After accumulating a small force in Indiana, he gathered them at Tippecanoe River in 1811, only to be defeated at the hands of the settlers. He allied his troops with the British the following year and suffered further defeat by the American forces in the War of 1812. He was killed after the Battle of Lake Erie as he headed north to Canada in retreat.

Andrew Jackson retaliated against the Creek raid on Alabama settlers by launching an attack at Horseshoe Bend and defeating them in a bloody battle. The Creeks in their turn ceded to the United States their territory in Alabama and along the Florida-Georgia border. Indians flooded into Florida to seek refuge.

In 1830 the states of Mississippi, Alabama and Georgia prohibited any settlement by Indians within their borders. In spite of Chief Justice John Calhoun's strong defense of Indian rights in the Supreme Court, Andrew Jackson passed the Indian Removal Act, creating Indian territory west of the Mississippi for all displaced Indians. The Choctaws ceded their land in Mississippi and spent the following three years making their way to the land allocated to them in Arkansas and Oklahoma. The Cherokees in Georgia were pushed out by white settlers and in return were given land in northeastern Oklahoma called Cherokee Strip. Those who refused to move were rounded up by General Winfield Scott and escorted west. The Trail of Tears, as it came to be called, took a year to complete, and by the end of the long and arduous trek, a quarter of the Indians had died. A small band of Cherokees were able to avoid the enforced migration and moved into North Carolina, where they were able to buy land in the mountains and reestablish a community and cultural tradition in isolation from white men.

In 1832 the Creeks ceded most of their land east of the Mississippi under duress, and when they refused to migrate they, too, were forced west, from 1836 to 1840. Two large settlements of Creek Indians formed the Creek Nation in 1839, but it ceased to exist in 1907 when Oklahoma was made a state. Other tribes that moved west began to settle and renew their cultural heritage. When coal was discovered in Indian Territory in the late 1880s and after the transcontinental railroad was completed, the grazing lands occupied by the Indians became desirable to white settlers

Above: A Seminole woman, photographed in 1957, demonstrates a method of grating kunti roots at the Big Cypress Reservation in Florida.

Left: A Seminole man skins a wild turkey in Florida in 1910. He is wearing the traditional knee-length appliqued shirt. The Seminoles developed a distinctive style of patchwork based on regular patterns of geometric designs that were sewn from strips of brightly colored fabric.

and once again they were encroached upon. By the end of the century, however, the US government began to tire of the Indian problem and eased up in its fight against the Indians. In 1889 a special commission granted 110 acres of land to every Cherokee individual who inhabited the Cherokee Strip.

In Florida a new mixed tribe called Seminoles, or runaways in Spanish, was formed of runaway slaves, Creeks and other refugee tribes. The Seminole Indians resisted the continued white settlement in Florida and in 1818 fought the First Seminole War against Andrew Jackson to protect their territory. They were pushed deeper south, into the Everglades, and in 1832 resisted the move to Indian Territory. From 1835 to 1842 they waged a second war in the struggle to retain what was left of their land. Although many of the tribe were removed to the west in 1856, a small number were able to cling to their land in Florida and to maintain a few isolated reservations.

Today the Indian population in the Southeast is only a small fraction of what it once was. Unlike their neighbors to the northeast, the southern tribes lived a more sedentary life and were less willing to give up their homes. They benefitted from larger populations and resisted removal from their homeland more than northern Indians, but to only marginally greater avail.

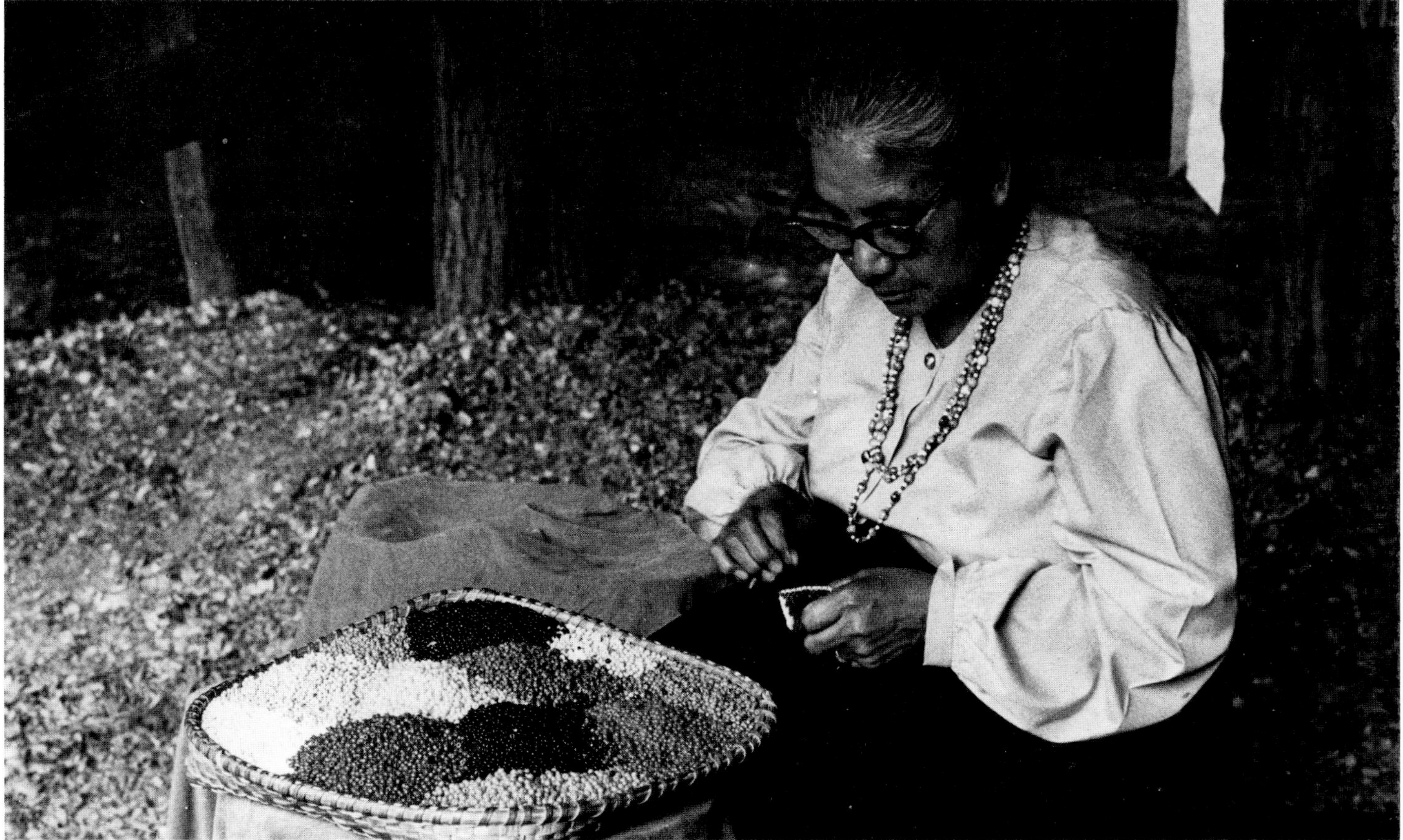

Top: A scene from daily life is reproduced in the Seminole Nation Museum in Wewoka, Oklahoma. The open-sided, thatch-covered chickee is the home for one family.

Above: Oconaluftee Indian village is an authentic recreation of an eighteenth-century Cherokee Indian community in North Carolina. The colorful Venetian beads were among the first trade goods introduced.

INDIANS OF THE PLAINS AND PRAIRIES

Between the Mississippi River and the Rocky Mountains, from Canada to southern Texas, ran a vast expanse of grasslands that teemed with buffalo. Before the seventeenth century, this territory was inhabited by a very small number of Indians who were bordered by the buffalo hunters to the west and farmers to the east. This was the home of the legendary redskin who became typified and immortalized in the stories of the Wild West, however inaccurate they were.

Big-game hunters roamed the boundless Plains and Prairies from about 10,000 to 4000 BC, until the land became too hot and dry to be habitable. Archaic cultures arrived a millennium later, only to be pushed out by more heat and drought. The western reaches of the Plains had sparse rainfall and remained dry and unsuitable for farming. In the flat, more fertile, eastern parts there were sufficient rivers,

Below: George Catlin, a writer and artist, was one of the earliest and most accurate of Indian painters. He was a New York portrait painter, but concentrated on painting Indians in their natural environment after a trip west in 1832. In this painting he pictured a Comanche about to lance to death an enemy Osage. The Comanches were the rulers of the western Plains and they were fanatical about war and horses. On horseback they were unbeatable, in part owing to their skills of breeding horses for speed and agility.

streams and rainfall to be conducive to agriculture. Farming was introduced here during the first 1000 years AD, and by 880 Indians on the eastern Plains were as reliant on farming as on hunting for survival. The populating of the Plains began in earnest around 1300 by cultures emigrating from other parts of the continent, seeking a new source of food, a better climate or more space. Within a few centuries the rapid settlement of the Northeast and Southeast by Europeans began forcing the westward movement first of the Indian, then of the settler.

Among the first Indians to settle the Plains and Prairies were the Pawnees and Wichitas, who moved from present-day Texas into Nebraska in the 1300s and prospered as farmers. In the north the Mandan tribe pushed west into the upper Missouri Valley, eventually establishing strong trade ties with the French. The Sioux (Dakota) and Crow came from the Great Lakes region and the Blackfoot from Canada, settling on the northern Plains. The Cheyenne Indians moved into the central Plains from the east and the Comanches came from the Great Basin to occupy the southern Plains.

The loosely organized tribes of the western Plains, typically the Crow, Blackfoot, Arapahoe, Cheyenne and Comanche, were wandering hunters. The eastern tribes, like the Sioux, Omaha and Missouri, were seminomadic farmers and hunters who lived in permanent villages between hunts. They returned to the villages at the beginning of summer, in time for the women to plant crops of corn, squash, beans and tobacco. Once this was accomplished, the tribe departed for a summer of hunting buffalo on the western Plains. They returned to harvest their crops and prepare the food for storage in concealed, underground pits.

Above: A portrait of Little Bluff, head chief of the Kiowas. The Kiowas were buffalo hunters, nomads of the Plains who came closest to matching the skill of the Comanches on horseback. These artful riders developed an unusual style of riding on the side of the horse, with one leg over the horse's back and one arm in a sling around the horse's neck, as a means of protection. Even when he slipped onto the side of the horse, the rider had two arms free and was still flexible enough to shoot arrows.

Indian Tribes of the Plains and Prairies

Arapahoe	Dakota (see Sioux)	Missouri	Sarsi
Arikara	Forest Potawatomi	Ojibwa	Sioux (Dakota)
Assiniboin	Gros Ventre	Omaha	Oglala
Atakapa	Hidatsa	Osage	Santee
Blackfoot	Iowa	Oto	Sisseton
Blood	Kansa	Pawnee	Teton
Piegan	Karankawa	Piankashaw	Yankton
Caddo	Kichai	Ponca	Teton Dakota
Cheyenne	Kiowa	Prairie	Wichita
Comanche	Mandan	Preoria	Wind River
Crow	Mesquakie	Quapaw	

Above: Sioux Indians parade through the center of Deadwood, South Dakota in the 1930s as part of the Days of '76 celebration.

Above right: Buffalo skins provided the canvas for the Plains Indian artist or historian, who recorded events in simple pictograph form. This 37-month Kiowa calendar covers the events of the years 1889 to 1892. Since there was no true form of writing and no universal set of symbols, the pictures could not always be understood.

The season closed with the Sun Dance, and the Plains Indians departed once again for an extended period of hunting.

Tribes of the western Prairies had never been farmers—they spent the year hunting and traveling in small bands, on foot. They carried their portable teepees and belongings on the dog-drawn, A-shaped travois wherever they went. The eastern Prairie tribes lived in log-framed, sod-covered earth lodges when they lived in villages, and like their western neighbors, lived in teepees when on the move. Buffalo hunting was the all-consuming passion of the Plains Indians and their lives were based on the hunt out of necessity for food. The Sun Dance at the end of the summer was a solemn affair for giving thanks to the sun and seeking the guidance of the guardian spirit for the future. Its purpose was also to gather the tribe and to prepare for the annual joint tribal hunt. This hunt was strictly organized and each member had a role to play. Scouts preceded the hunting party, warriors kept guard in the rear and police were assigned to maintain order. The women were responsible for packing the belongings, in keeping with their role of managing the household.

The buffalo hunt itself was conducted on foot in the early days and was an extremely dangerous enterprise in which many lives were lost. The weapons were bows and arrows and spears. The two methods of attack were to surround the herd, either with fire or a corral, and kill the buffalos or to draw the herd to the edge of a cliff and stampede it from behind. Carcasses of buffalo were carried home on the travois, and the end of the hunt was celebrated with a feast of roasted or raw buffalo meat. The animals were dis-

membered by the women and every part was put to use. Hides were tanned and made into teepees, blankets and clothing; hair was used for weaving; horns and bones were carved into utensils; dried manure pats were used for fuel; and the belly was turned into a cooking pot. The remaining meat was hung to dry or pounded with other ingredients into pemmican, the basis of the Plains Indian diet.

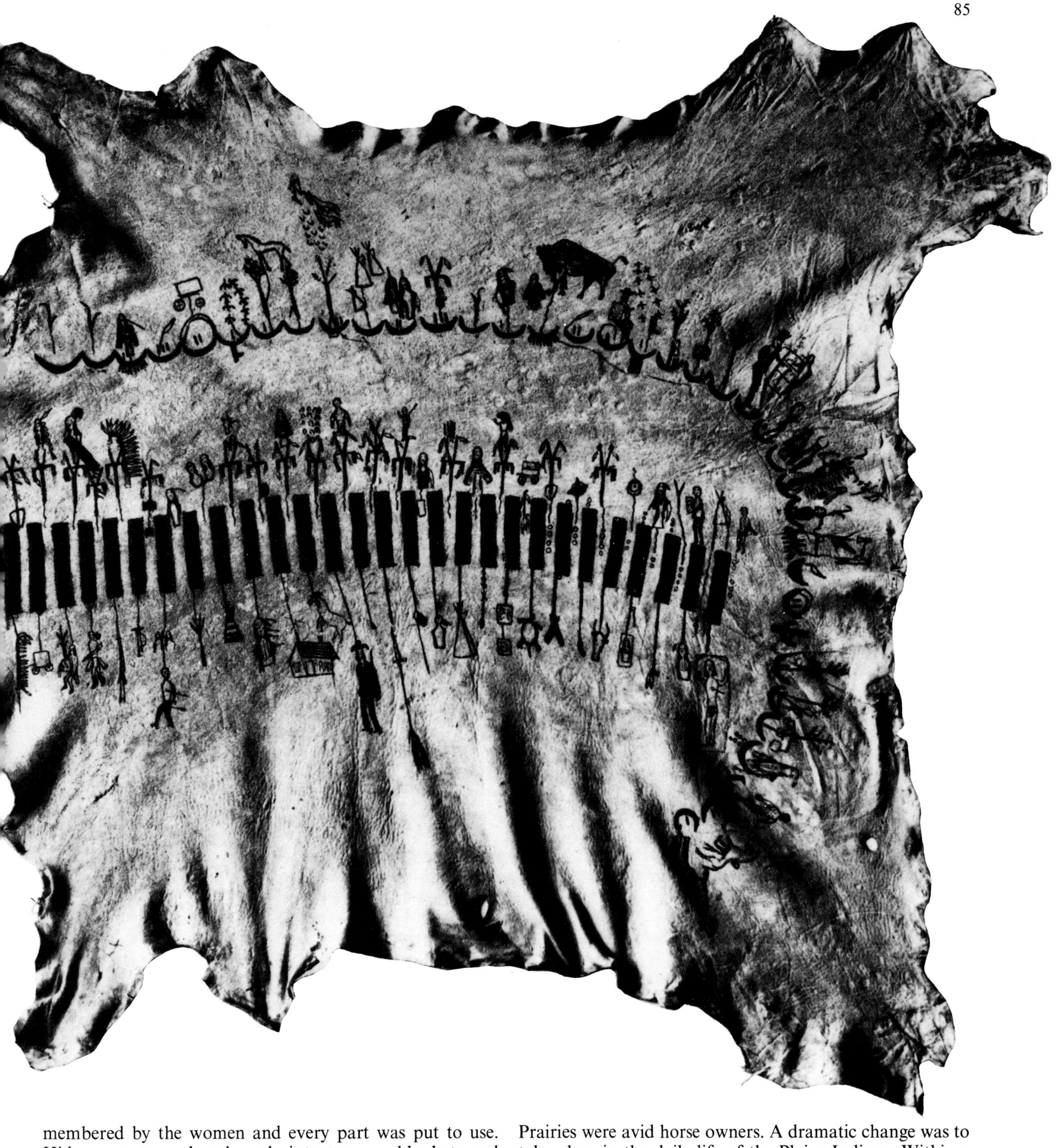

In 1541 the Spanish conquistadores brought the horse to North America via Mexico. In the 1600s Southwestern Indians began supplying the Plains Indians with horses through trade and by 1750 most Indians on the Plains and Prairies were avid horse owners. A dramatic change was to take place in the daily life of the Plains Indians. Within a short space of time they were exceptional riders and breeders, especially the Comanches, who learned to breed a fleet-footed pony that was unmatched for swiftness in battle. It was the man's role to breed and care for the horses, but in the Blackfoot tribe, women also owned herds. Comanche women competed with men hunting on horseback. Transportation was vastly improved because the horse was capable of carrying much heavier loads on the travois than the dog was. Hunting was far easier on horse-

Below: Charles H Russell was a prolific artist who painted the Plains Indians in action. This detail from *Jumped* depicts a surprise attack of Indians on white settlers. Such hit and run warfare was the trademark of the Indians.

Below: This photograph of a teepee was taken in the late 1860s or early 1870s. It was the lodge of Chief Little Big Mouth, thought to be a Cheyenne. In the Northeast the tepee was made of bark; in the Plains it was made of buffalo hide. Women sewed the skins together with sinew, using about 15 hides for a small teepee or as many as 50 for a main, ceremonial teepee. The skins were stretched over three or four main poles that were supported by 20 or more smaller poles. The Plains home was easily disassembled for travel and the main poles provided the frame for the travois.

back, encouraging the Plains Indians, especially the Crow and Cheyenne, to abandon the village and to become even more nomadic in their ways. With this newfound mobility, hunting could be accomplished more quickly and there was more time for war. Horse raiding became a common event and it lasted for weeks at a time. This was the means of gaining wealth and of increasing one's social status in the tribe.

A large number of different tribes occupied the Plains, with each speaking its own language. To overcome the language barrier the Plains Indians developed a sign language by using gestures that could be understood by all. In spite of the many differences, daily life of the Indians was much the same in this territory. Tribes numbered anywhere from 1000 to 10,000 in population and were headed by one or more chiefs who were selected on the basis of great deeds in war, but who had no real authority. On the eastern Plains families organized themselves by clan, and kinship was based on descent from either the father or mother. Compared to Indians of the eastern forests, these tribes were loosely organized. They were bound together by their customs. For the most part, ceremonies (which varied from tribe to tribe) were not complex and attendance was not mandatory. The Sun Dance, the main celebration, united the tribe for the annual hunt. Many tribes had select societies, some based on age and some not, that provided tribal unity by keeping order, preserving and passing on traditions and organizing the social life.

Indians of most of North America were preoccupied with war in addition to hunting, but for most tribes warfare was a sporting activity, albeit serious, that involved only minor skirmishes. It was the arrival of the white settlers that elevated war into wholesale bloodshed and introduced the gun that Indians reserved as their weapon for war. Indians fought among themselves to protect their territory, to keep their enemies at bay and to settle disputes when they could not settle them in the council. War was usually the means of proving one's bravery and of accumulating coup

Above: An Indian travois display from a Cheyenne pageant in 1951. The A-shaped arrangement of poles carried the family's belongings. When the horse was introduced to the Indian, it meant that a bigger travois could be designed than the one that had been used with dogs.

Below: Seven Indian reservations in South Dakota sponsor sun dances and fairs in the summer, to which visitors are welcome.

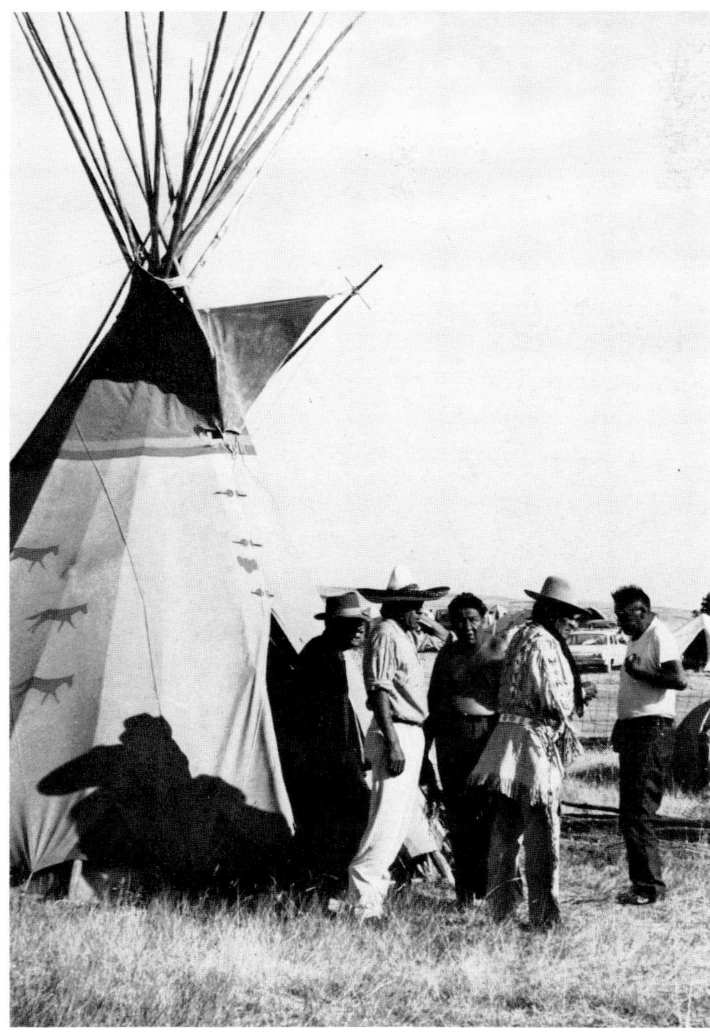

Above: George Catlin, the great American painter of the West, met Steep Wind, a Sans Arc Sioux chief, during his 1832 visit to South Dakota and painted him in full military regalia.

Right: Charles M Russell painted these Indian scouts in Montana, on the lookout for whites. Indians were protective of their territory and were ever watchful for intruders and enemies.

points to improve one's standing in the community. Deeds of war were assigned various points, and in most cases bravery was far more important than killing and savagery. Sioux and Cheyenne warriors earned more points by touching a live enemy with a coup stick than by killing or scalp taking. The highest honors accorded a Blackfoot warrior were for taking an enemy's weapon, then for taking his scalp, and then his horse. Feathers were awarded for achievements and were marked to indicate the deed that earned them. In some tribes victory after battle was celebrated with scalp dances, when warriors were given the chance to recount their brave deeds in detail. The fearless Comanches were infamous raiders who pursued war for its glory and struck terror in their victims. If prisoners were taken, they were in most cases adopted into the tribe that captured them, unaccompanied by the savage treatment that prevailed among eastern tribes. Some tribes allowed women to participate in battle.

Chastity was a virtue according to most Plains Indians and they were less liberal about premarital sexual activity than eastern tribes. Parents were usually responsible for making matches, but there was flexibility in this practice. The value of the bride was determined by the number of horses her prospective husband was willing to give her

Above: Buffalo meat hangs to dry in front of an Arapahoe camp in 1870.

Right: A Crow Indian burial platform, out of reach of animals.

Next page: A Charles Bird King portrait, painted in 1821, of a Pawnee delegation to Washington, the nation's capital.

father, and the value of the husband was defined by his horsemanship and his success as a raider. The marriage itself was simple and straightforward. Because the mortality rate of males was high, resulting in a low ratio of men to women, men were encouraged to be polygamous, especially if they were wealthy. The woman's workload was heavy and having several wives eased that burden.

Birth took place in the teepee and was assisted by a midwife. It was an occasion for celebration because the child was valued highly among the Plains tribes. Sioux children were assigned a second set of parents to look after them, and all children were raised in loving environments with very little of the strict discipline practiced elsewhere. The onset of menstruation in young girls was yet another occasion for celebration, especially among the Sioux and Cheyenne, because it marked the entry into womanhood. Thereafter the girl was isolated from the rest of the village during her period, out of fear that she would taint others with evil spirits. During those times she received instruction from her mother in the traditional skills, such as painting, beadwork and porcupine quill embroidery. Women kept records of their achievements, and during the Sun Dance ceremony competed against each other to show off their abilities. A good wife was one who was accomplished at crafts and good at tanning.

Plains Indian art was less elaborate than art produced in other regions of North America. Painting was popular, but only the men were permitted to paint representational scenes while women were restricted to geometrical drawings. When glass beads were brought over from Europe, Indians traded eagerly for them. They loved the bright colors, which were far more vivid than the shells and seeds they were already using. The beads were much easier to sew and were applied to entire garments, usually reserved for ceremonial use.

The Vision Quest was common to many tribes of North America, and it was the means by which a Plains Indian boy was initiated into manhood at puberty. After purifying

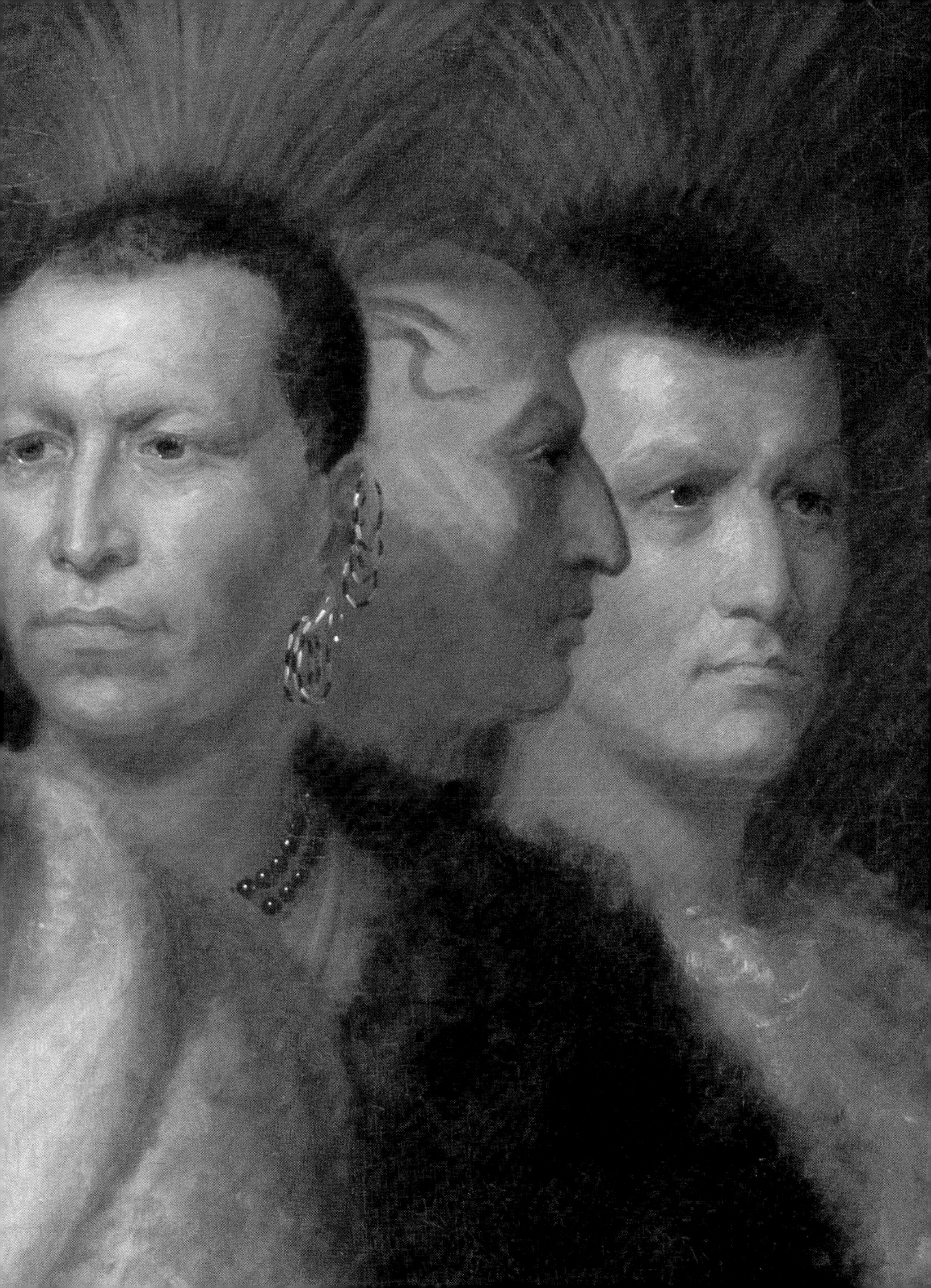

Left: Crow chief Plenty Coup and his forces fought with the US Army against the Sioux. Crow warriors were noted for their elaborate dress and long hair.

Above: Cheyenne Indians skin a cow, provided by the government when hunting buffalo became no longer practical, in 1887.

himself in the sweathouse, he climbed naked into a dark pit, where he remained in isolation for several days, fasting and waiting for his personal guardian spirit to come to him. Throughout his life, whenever he was in hardship and needed the help of his spirit, the man would undergo another similar vigil. Upon completing his initiation, the youth assembled a medicine bag of a variety of items with magical properties that he would carry with him into battle. In some tribes, a boy's entry into manhood took place when he had killed his first buffalo.

The Plains culture was shortlived. Although the Plains Indian made a valiant effort to preserve his way of life, the white man was too strong and too unaccommodating to tolerate Indian ways. The Indian was once again swept aside in the quest for land.

In the effort to open up the West to the white man, Thomas Jefferson sent Meriwether Lewis and William Clark on an expedition in 1804 across North America to the Pacific coast to encourage trade with the Indians. The venture was a success and was followed by an influx of traders and trappers, who in themselves did not pose a great threat to the Indians. They did, however, introduce the Indians in the West to whiskey and new diseases that were to prove disastrous. A smallpox epidemic in 1830 virtually wiped out the Mandan tribe in the northern Plains.

Up to about 1850 the plains were still Indian domain. Settlers were not very interested in living in that remote inhospitable wilderness. For the white man the Plains and Prairies were hunting grounds and they were a barrier to the far West. The creation of the Oregon Trail in the 1840s opened up migration and brought about the establishment of forts along the way to protect the travelers. But in 1869 the completion of the transcontinental railroad, connecting the two coasts, changed everything and ushered in a rash of settlement by miners, farmers and cattlemen. Once a network of railroads had been established, the Plains became instantly attractive. With the help of the railroad, buffalo hunting as a sport became popular, and hunters were heard to boast of the large numbers they could kill in an hour. By 1870 the buffalo population was reduced to less than one third of its original size. Thirty short years later the bison numbered only a tiny fraction of that and faced extinction. Loss of the buffalo alone was enough to guarantee the demise of Plains Indian cultures because it had been a way of life as well as a means of subsistence.

The period from 1850 to 1890 was one of treaty signing, treaty breaking, clashes with the white settlers and wars with the Army. In 1851 the Plains Indians signed their first treaty with the federal government, allowing access to their territory but not realizing the government's intention to limit the Indian's range. Chiefs signed the treaties, often under the inducement of whiskey, but they were powerless to enforce them. Fierce fighting and bloody slaughter were inevitable as Indians were forced off their land, into new and strange territory, where supplies for food were rapidly diminishing from overhunting.

In many cases the Army struck with the slightest excuse. When a band of Sioux were discovered to have killed a sick cow for food, the Army attacked and opened up three decades of war in which the Indians were often victorious. When Colonel John Chivington attacked and massacred Black Kettle and his Cheyennes at Sand Creek, Colorado in 1864, he sparked retaliation by the Indians of all the central Plains. The establishment of several Army forts

(Text continues on page 114)

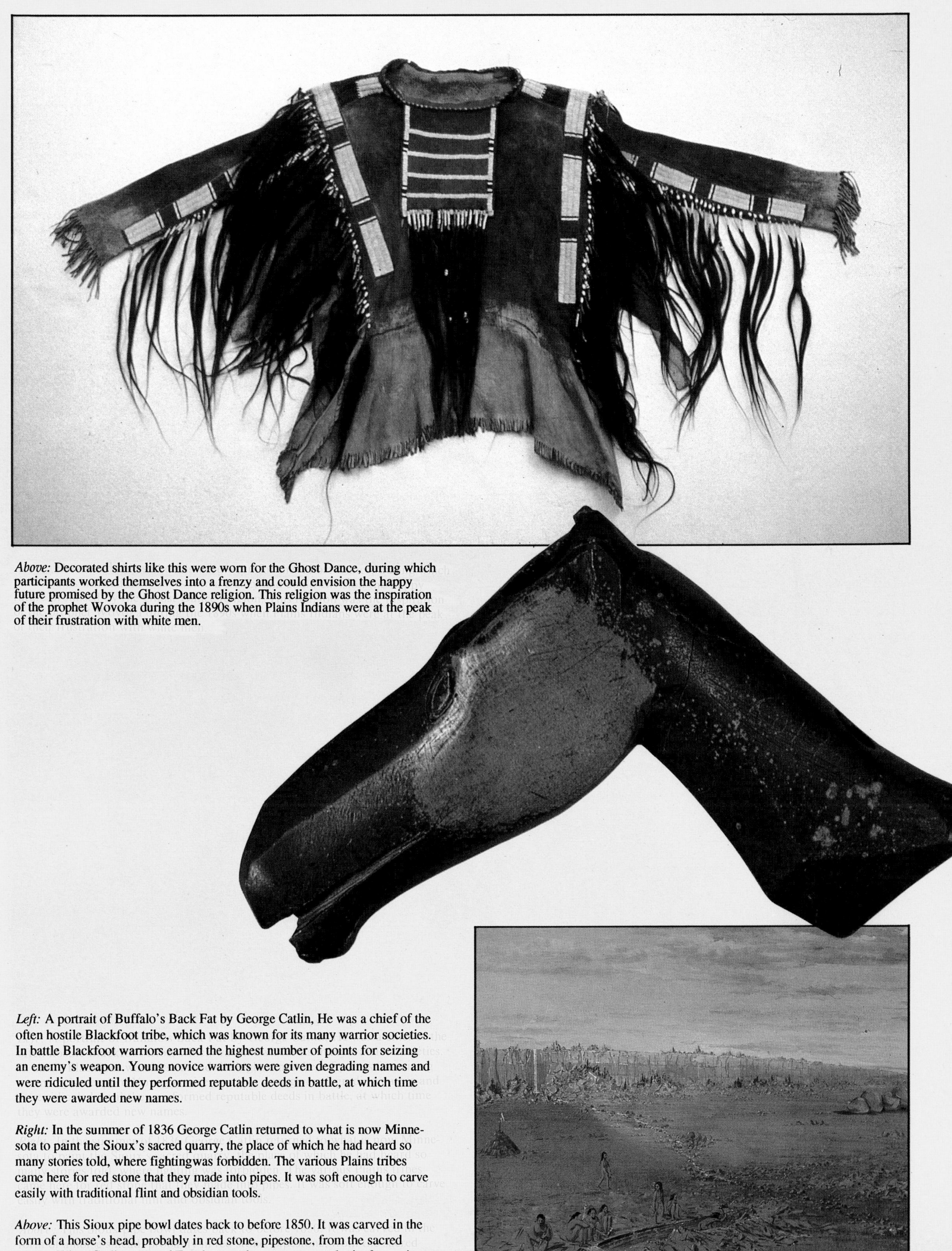

Above: Decorated shirts like this were worn for the Ghost Dance, during which participants worked themselves into a frenzy and could envision the happy future promised by the Ghost Dance religion. This religion was the inspiration of the prophet Wovoka during the 1890s when Plains Indians were at the peak of their frustration with white men.

Left: A portrait of Buffalo's Back Fat by George Catlin, He was a chief of the often hostile Blackfoot tribe, which was known for its many warrior societies. In battle Blackfoot warriors earned the highest number of points for seizing an enemy's weapon. Young novice warriors were given degrading names and were ridiculed until they performed reputable deeds in battle, at which time they were awarded new names.

Right: In the summer of 1836 George Catlin returned to what is now Minnesota to paint the Sioux's sacred quarry, the place of which he had heard so many stories told, where fightingwas forbidden. The various Plains tribes came here for red stone that they made into pipes. It was soft enough to carve easily with traditional flint and obsidian tools.

Above: This Sioux pipe bowl dates back to before 1850. It was carved in the form of a horse's head, probably in red stone, pipestone, from the sacred quarry. When Catlin returned East he sent the stone to a geologist for testing, and the newfound mineral was named Catlinite.

Above: Quanah Parker, chief of the Kwahadi Comanches, was the son of a Comanche father and a white captive, Cynthia Ann Parker. He led a combined force of Kiowas, Comanches, Cheyennes and Arapahos against white settlements at Adobe Walls and Palo Duro Canyon in northern Texas in retaliation against constant encroachment by buffalo hunters on territory that had been guaranteed to the Indians. Quanah Parker and his forces were finally forced to surrender in 1875. This occurred at Adobe Walls on the North Canadian River and was a crushing blow to Indian morale.

Right: Wanada Parker, on the left, was the daughter of Quañah Parker. These two young Comanche girls were photographed at the Kiowa Reservation in Oklahoma sometime between 1891 and 1893. Like the Eskimos, Plains Indians loved children and rarely punished them.

Next page: Armed with bloody weapons and fresh scalps, a band of Teton Sioux perform a scalp dance. Among the Plains tribes honors were accorded for bravery in battle. Coup points were awarded for touching a live enemy with a coup stick. Stealing a horse, seizing a weapon, killing the enemy, beheading or scalping were all rewarded. Scalping was common among all North American Indian tribes, but was not regarded as the highest achievement of battle. The scalp dance was a celebration of the belief that the powers of the dead were passed onto the living and took place after the victorious war party returned home. At this time warriors gave a detailed account of their deeds for the benefit of the rest of the tribe, but they were scorned if they gave false reports or if they exaggerated their achievements. The scalp dance was also the opportunity to mourn the men who had been lost in battle.

In Defense of their Homes

We have been south and suffered a great deal down there. Many have died of diseases which we have no name for. Our hearts looked and longed for this country where we were born. There are only a few of us left, and we only wanted a little ground, where we could live. We left our lodges standing, and ran away in the night. The troops followed us. I rode out and told the troops we did not want to fight; we only wanted to go north, and if they would let us alone we would kill no one. The only reply we got was a volley. After that we had to fight our way, but we killed none who did not fire at us first. My brother, Dull Knife, took one-half of the band and surrendered near Fort Robinson. . . . They gave up their guns, and then the whites killed them all.
—Little Wolf of the Northern Cheyennes
(d. 1879)

No white person or persons shall be permitted to settle upon or occupy any portion of the territory, or without the consent of the Indians to pass through the same.
—Treaty of 1868

All Indians must dance, everywhere, keep on dancing. Pretty soon in next spring Great Spirit come. He bring back all game of every kind. The game be thick everywhere. All dead Indians come back and live again. They all be strong just like young men, be young again. Old blind Indian see again and get young and have fine time. When Great Spirit comes this way, then all the Indians go to mountains, high up away from whites. Whites can't hurt Indians then. Then while Indians way up high, big flood comes like water and all white people die, get drowned. After that, water go away and then nobody but Indians everywhere and game all kinds thick. Then medicine man tell Indians to send word to all Indians to keep up dancing and the good time will come. Indians who don't dance, who don't believe in this word, will grow little, just about a foot high, and stay that way. Some of them will be turned into wood and be burned in fire.
—Wovoka, the Paiute Messiah
(d. 1890)

All we ask is to be allowed to live, and live in peace. . . . We bowed to the will of the Great Father and went south. There we found a Cheyenne cannot live. So we came home. Better it was, we thought, to die fighting than to perish of sickness. . . . You may kill me here; but you cannot make me go back. We will not go. The only way to get us there is to come in here with clubs and knock us on the head, and drag us out and take us down there dead.
—Dull Knife of the Northern Cheyennes
(d. 1879)

Left: Red Cloud, chief of the Oglala Sioux, and his warriors forced the US Army to give up its forts along the Bozeman Trail in 1868. This was the only acknowledged Indian victory over the US government.

Below: Red Cloud's delegation to Washington to meet with President Grant included (l to r) Red Dog, Little Wound, John Bridgeman (interpreter), Red Cloud, American Horse and Red Shirt.

Below: In 1908 Charles Russell painted *The Medicine Man* directing a move across the Plains, a regular occurrence for buffalo-hunting Indians. Women, children and elders traveled in the middle of the party while guards remained at the rear to protect against enemy attack. Each family was responsible for its own belongings, which they hauled by travois or on their backs. Even with the horse, progress was slow and only five miles or so could be covered each day.

Voices of Indian Frustration

You have driven me from the East to this place, and I have been here two thousand years or more. . . . My friends, if you took me away from this land it would be very hard for me. I wish to die in this land. I wish to be an old man here. . . . I have not wished to give even a part of it to the Great Father. Though he were to give me a million dollars I would not give him this land. . . . When people want to slaughter cattle they drive them along until they get them to a corral, and then they slaughter them. So it was with us. . . . My children have been exterminated; my brother has been killed.

—*Standing Bear of the Poncas (d. 1879)*

The soldiers came to the borders of the village and forced us across the Niobrara to the other side, just as one would drive a herd of ponies; and the soldiers pushed us on until we came to the Platte River. They drove us on in advance just as if we were a herd of ponies, and I said, "If I have to go, I'll go to that land. Let the soldiers go away, our women are afraid of them." And so I reached the Warm Land. We found the land there was bad and we were dying one after another, and we said, "What man will take pity on us?" And our animals died. Oh, it was very hot. "This land is truly sickly, and we'll be apt to die here, and we hope the Great Father will take us back again." That is what we said. There were one hundred of us died there.

—*White Eagle of the Poncas (d. 1879)*

I want to know what you are doing on this road. You scare all the buffalo away. I want to hunt in this place. I want you to turn back from here. If you don't, I will fight you again. I want you to leave what you have got here, and turn back from here. I am your friend.

—*Sitting Bull (d. 1890)*

We want no white men here. The Black Hills belong to me. If the whites try to take them, I will fight.

—*Sitting Bull*

One does not sell the earth upon which the people walk.

—*Crazy Horse (d. 1877)*

The whites were always trying to make the Indians give up their life and live like white men—go to farming, work hard and do as they did—and the Indians did not know how to do that, and did not want to anyway. . . . If the Indians had tried to make the whites live like them, the whites would have resisted, and it was the same way with many Indians.

—*Big Eagle of the Santee Sioux (d. 1863)*

You have driven away our game and our means of livelihood out of the country, until now we have nothing left that is valuable except the hills that you ask us to give up. . . . The earth is full of minerals of all kinds, and on the earth the ground is covered with forests of heavy pine, and when we give these up to the Great Father we know that we give up the last thing that is valuable either to us or the white people.

—*White Ghost (d. 1876)*

Left: Rain in the Face, a Hunkpapa Sioux, killed Captain Tom Custer, brother of Lieutenant Colonel George Custer, at the Battle of Little Big Horn. Following this great Indian victory of 1876, Rain in the Face ate his victim's heart (a grisly practice sometimes carried out on captives) in revenge for a humiliation inflicted earlier by the younger Custer.

Below left: The Hunkpapa war chief Gall fought alongside Crazy Horse, an Oglala Sioux, at Little Big Horn and helped annihilate Custer's force. The Hunkpapa were a subtribe of the Teton Sioux.

Below: Sitting Bull was a medicine man of the Hunkpapa and a great warrior who became chief of his tribe. He directed the Sioux in their victory against Custer but withdrew afterwards with his troops to Canada in order to avoid being rounded up. He was killed several years later, in 1890, trying to avoid arrest at Standing Rock Reservation.

Above: Red Horse, a Sioux Indian, painted a crude account of the Battle at Little Big Horn showing the mutilation of Custer's troops. This is surely a different version from those painted by white artists.

Above: A pile of horse skulls and other bones bear silent testimony to the bloody battle in which Custer and his troops were defeated. Custer had been looking for a victory that he believed would lead him to glory and make him a good candidate for the Democratic party in the presidential election that was to be held later that year. Only Comanche, Captain Keogh's horse, was left alive on the Custer battlefield and 260 whites were dead or mortally wounded.

Below: This detail from Red Horse's colorful 1881 pictograph shows the Miniconjou Sioux warriors mounted on horseback, armed with spears and lances, as they prepare to attack the Seventh Cavalry under Lieutenant Colonel George Custer.

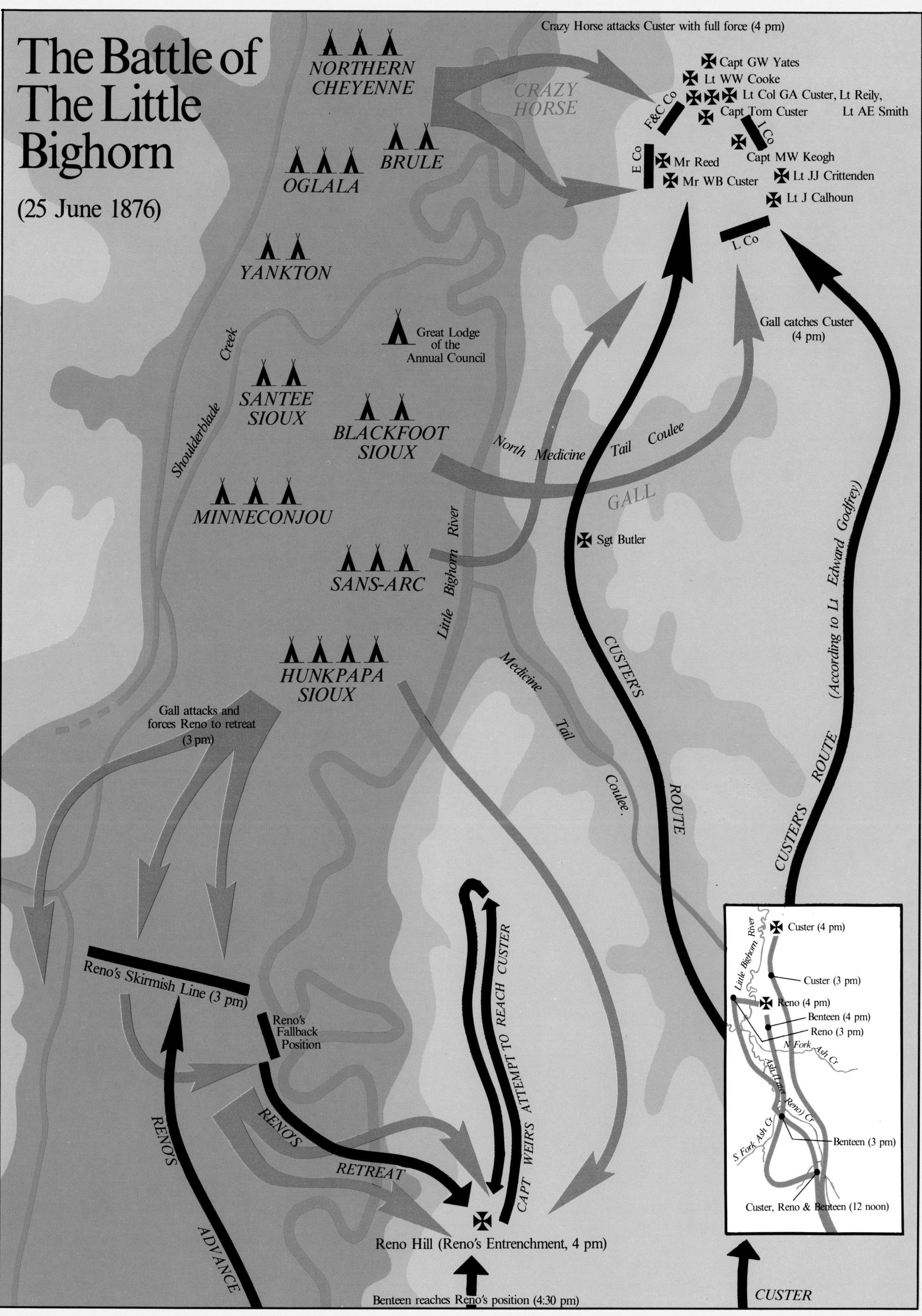

The Battle of The Little Bighorn
(25 June 1876)
Crazy Horse attacks Custer with full force (4 pm)
NORTHERN CHEYENNE
CRAZY HORSE
BRULE
OGLALA
YANKTON
Great Lodge of the Annual Council
SANTEE SIOUX
BLACKFOOT SIOUX
MINNECONJOU
SANS-ARC
HUNKPAPA SIOUX
Shoulderblade Creek
Little Bighorn River
North Medicine Tail Coulee
GALL
Medicine Tail Coulee
Capt GW Yates
Lt WW Cooke
Lt Col GA Custer, Lt Reily,
Capt Tom Custer
Lt AE Smith
F&C Co
I Co
E Co
Mr Reed
Mr WB Custer
Capt MW Keogh
Lt JJ Crittenden
Lt J Calhoun
L Co
Gall catches Custer (4 pm)
Sgt Butler
CUSTER'S ROUTE
CUSTER'S ROUTE (According to Lt Edward Godfrey)
Gall attacks and forces Reno to retreat (3 pm)
Reno's Skirmish Line (3 pm)
Reno's Fallback Position
RENO'S ADVANCE
RENO'S RETREAT
CAPT WEIR'S ATTEMPT TO REACH CUSTER
Reno Hill (Reno's Entrenchment, 4 pm)
Benteen reaches Reno's position (4:30 pm)
CUSTER
Little Bighorn River
Custer (4 pm)
Custer (3 pm)
Reno (4 pm)
Benteen (4 pm)
Reno (3 pm)
N Fork Ash Cr
Ash (Later Reno) Cr
S Fork Ash Cr
Benteen (3 pm)
Custer, Reno & Benteen (12 noon)

US Commissioners and Delegations of Sioux Chiefs Visiting Washington 15 October 1888

PINE RIDGE AGENCY DELEGATION

43. Dog Back.
44. Standing Soldier, 1st Lieut Police.
45. Yellow Bear.
46. Little Hawk.
47. Little Wound.
48. Little Chief (Cheyenne).
49. Pretty Lance.
50. Standing Elk (Cheyenne).
51. Fast Thunder.
52. No Flesh.
53. American Horse.
54. Capt George Sword, Police Force.
55. Plenty Bears.
56. Benjamin Rowland, Interpreter.
57. Philip Wells, Interpreter.
58. Col H D Gallager, Agent at Pine Ridge.

CHEYENNE RIVER, CROW CREEK, AND LOWER BRULE DELEGATIONS

59. White Ghost.
60. Drifting Goose.
61. Bowed Head.
62. Little Bear.
63. Spotted Elk.
64. Crow Eagle.
65. White Swan.
66. Charger.
67. Spotted Eagle.
68. Swift Bird.
69. Little No-heart.
70. Narcisse Narcell.
71. William Larabee, Interpreter.
72. Dr C E McChesney, Agent at Cheyenne River.
73. Mark Wells, Interpreter.
74. Capt William Carpenter, Police Force.
Maj W W Anderson, Agent Crow Creek and Lower Brule.
76. Capt Fire-thunder, Police Force.
7. Alex Rencontre, Interpreter.
78. Medicine Bull.
79. Bull Head.
80. Wizi.

ROSEBUD AGENCY DELEGATION

11. Ugly Wild-Horse.
12. Pretty Eagle.
13. He-Dog.
14. Good Voice.
15. Quick Bear.
16. Black Wolf.
17. Swift Bear.
18. King Thunder.
19. Two Strike.
20. Gray Eagle-tail.
21. Sky Bull.
22. Red Fish.
23. Yellow Hair.
24. Eagle Horse.
25. Thomas Flood, Interpreter.
26. Col L F Spencer, Agent at Rosebud.

STANDING ROCK AGENCY DELEGATION

27. Sitting Bull.
28. Steph Two-bear.
29. Bear's Rib.
30. Thunder Hawk.
31. High Eagle.
32. Big Head.
33. Mad Bear.
34. Gray Eagle.
35. Hairy Chin.
36. Walking Eagle.
37. High Bear.
38. Fire Heart.
39. John Grasse.
40. Gaul.
41. Louis Primean, Interpreter.
42. Maj James A McLaughlin, Agent at Standing Rock.

1. Capt R H Pratt, Commissioner.
2. Rev Wm J Cleveland, Commissioner.
3. Hon John V Wright, Commissioner.
4. Hon Jno Oberly, Commissioner of Indian Affairs.
5. Gov L K Church, of Dakota.
6. Hon Edmond Rice, Minn.
7. R V Belt, Indian Department.
8. Col R S Gardner, Inspector.
9. Col S F Tappan.
10. G L Stevick.

Left: Big Foot, chief of the Sioux, lies dead in the snow in the aftermath of the Battle at Wounded Knee in 1890, where he surrendered to the US Army. When officers attempted to seize all Indian weapons, they opened up a bloody and deadly confrontation that shocked most Americans. It was the last of the Indian wars in North America.

Below: Big Foot's band of Miniconjou Sioux gather for a grass dance at the Cheyenne River in South Dakota in better days, August 1890.

Right: Most of Big Foot's warriors were killed in the Battle at Wounded Knee. Women and children were shot down at close quarters in the massacre, and all were buried later in a common grave.

Previous page: St Mary Lake, in northern Montana, lies just south of the Canadian border and forms part of the boundary between Glacier National Park and the Blackfoot reservation. A contemporary Blackfoot homesite stretches along the shores of the lake.

Above: Contemporary Indian children participate in the Tulsa Pow Wow, held during the summer in Tulsa, Oklahoma. Only about half of the tribes today live on official reservations, and they are making a real effort at revitalizing their cultural heritage. Pow wows are common on reservations and, although tourists are welcomed spectators, these events are primarily an opportunity for various tribes to come together over common issues and to practice their traditions.

Right: Pow wows, festivals and centennials are held throughout the summer in South Dakota to commemorate Sioux culture and history. Visitors interested in Sioux history can learn more about this tribe through special events, museum exhibits and cultural centers across the state.

and his remaining band escaped into Canada. He returned to the United States six months later to surrender to government troops.

In 1889 the Indian Commission promised, among other things, food rations for the hungry Sioux and never delivered them. Once-enemy tribes came together, united in their grievances and frustration with the US government. They became increasingly hostile, refused to return to the reservation and slipped into the outlying badlands. As a precaution against the outbreak of war, the government prepared its troops. In response partly to the scarcity of food, the Indians increased their raids and plundering. Sitting Bull was killed on 15 December after he was arrested

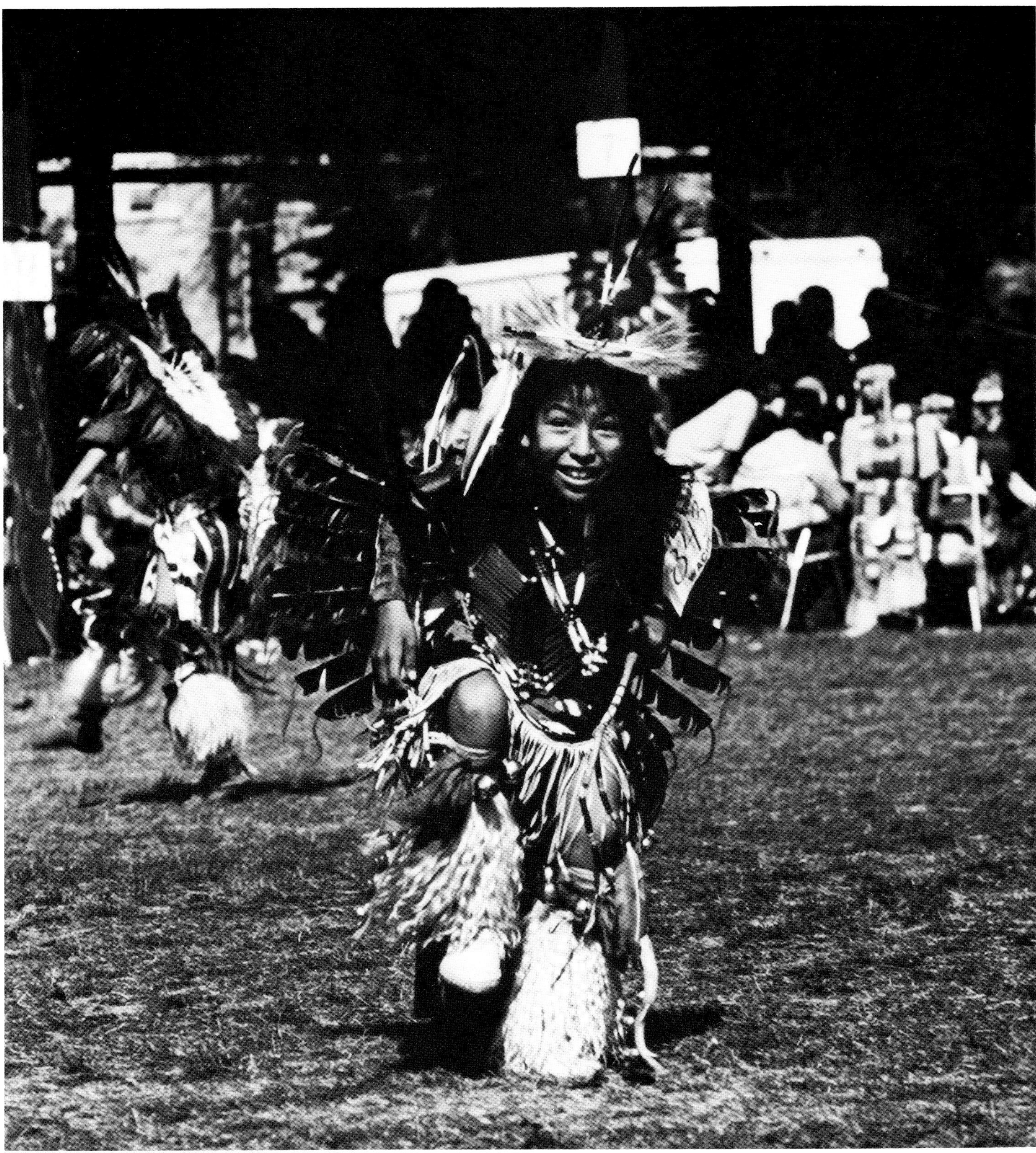

to prevent his escape from the agency. By this time Ghost Dance religion, which many Indians felt required the destruction of the whites, was reaching fever pitch. Chief Big Foot fled with his forces, was caught and put in a camp near Wounded Knee. The Army surrounded the camp on 29 December 1890 and searched for arms. In spite of General Miles' attempts to avoid bloodshed, the breaking point had been reached and 120 desperate Indians turned on the cavalry. The engagement continued as Army troops in their turn slaughtered men, women and children in the last major armed conflict that was to take place between the Indians and white man on the Plains and Prairies of the western United States.

The public reacted with horror at the irresponsibility of the Army, but the white man had succeeded in resolving the Indian problem and clearing the land at great expense to both sides. By the end of the century industrialization had taken over the West and completely changed the face of the Plains.

In 1973 a group of 200 militant Indians occupied the village of Wounded Knee in South Dakota in response to the accumulated injustices suffered by American Indians. Before their eventual surrender, after a little more than two months of occupation, they had lost two Indians and nearly destroyed the village, a bitter reminder of the way things had once been.

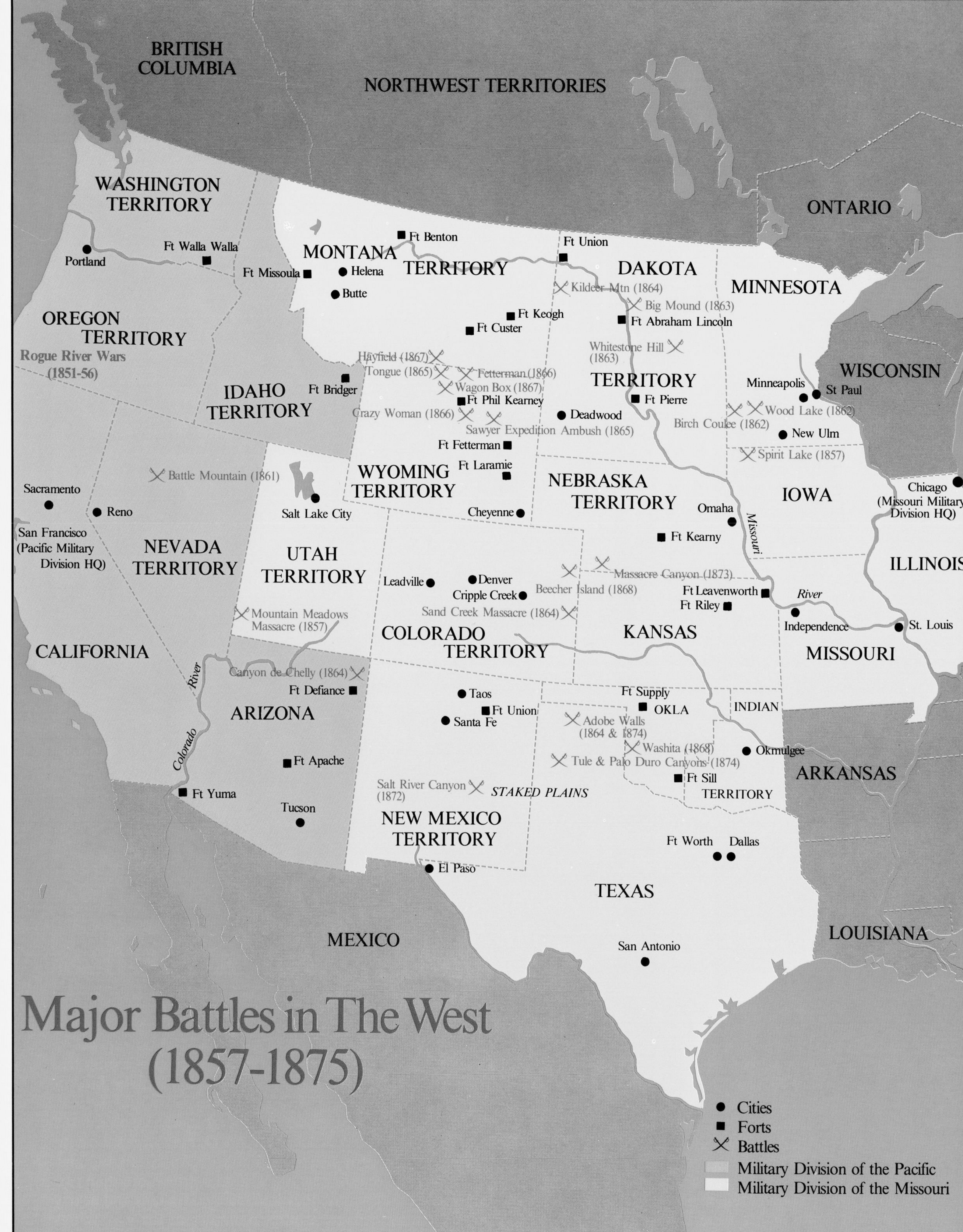

BRITISH COLUMBIA
NORTHWEST TERRITORIES
ONTARIO
WASHINGTON TERRITORY
Portland
Ft Walla Walla
MONTANA TERRITORY
Ft Benton
Ft Missoula
Helena
Butte
Ft Union
DAKOTA TERRITORY
MINNESOTA
Kildeer Mtn (1864)
Big Mound (1863)
Ft Keogh
Ft Abraham Lincoln
Ft Custer
OREGON TERRITORY
Rogue River Wars (1851-56)
Hayfield (1867)
Tongue (1865)
Fetterman (1866)
Wagon Box (1867)
Ft Phil Kearney
Crazy Woman (1866)
Sawyer Expedition Ambush (1865)
Whitestone Hill (1863)
Ft Pierre
Deadwood
WISCONSIN
Minneapolis
St Paul
Wood Lake (1862)
Birch Coulee (1862)
New Ulm
IDAHO TERRITORY
Ft Bridger
Ft Fetterman
Ft Laramie
Spirit Lake (1857)
Battle Mountain (1861)
WYOMING TERRITORY
NEBRASKA TERRITORY
IOWA
Sacramento
Reno
Salt Lake City
Cheyenne
Omaha
Chicago (Missouri Military Division HQ)
San Francisco (Pacific Military Division HQ)
NEVADA TERRITORY
UTAH TERRITORY
Ft Kearny
Missouri
ILLINOIS
Leadville
Denver
Cripple Creek
Massacre Canyon (1873)
Beecher Island (1868)
Ft Leavenworth
Ft Riley
River
Mountain Meadows Massacre (1857)
Sand Creek Massacre (1864)
Independence
St. Louis
CALIFORNIA
COLORADO TERRITORY
KANSAS
MISSOURI
River
Canyon de Chelly (1864)
Ft Defiance
Taos
Ft Union
Santa Fe
Ft Supply
OKLA
INDIAN
ARIZONA
Adobe Walls (1864 & 1874)
Washita (1868)
Okmulgee
Tule & Palo Duro Canyons (1874)
Colorado
Ft Apache
Ft Sill
ARKANSAS
Ft Yuma
Salt River Canyon (1872)
STAKED PLAINS
TERRITORY
Tucson
NEW MEXICO TERRITORY
Ft Worth
Dallas
El Paso
TEXAS
MEXICO
LOUISIANA
San Antonio
Cities
Forts
Battles
Military Division of the Pacific
Military Division of the Missouri

Major Battles in The West (1857-1875)

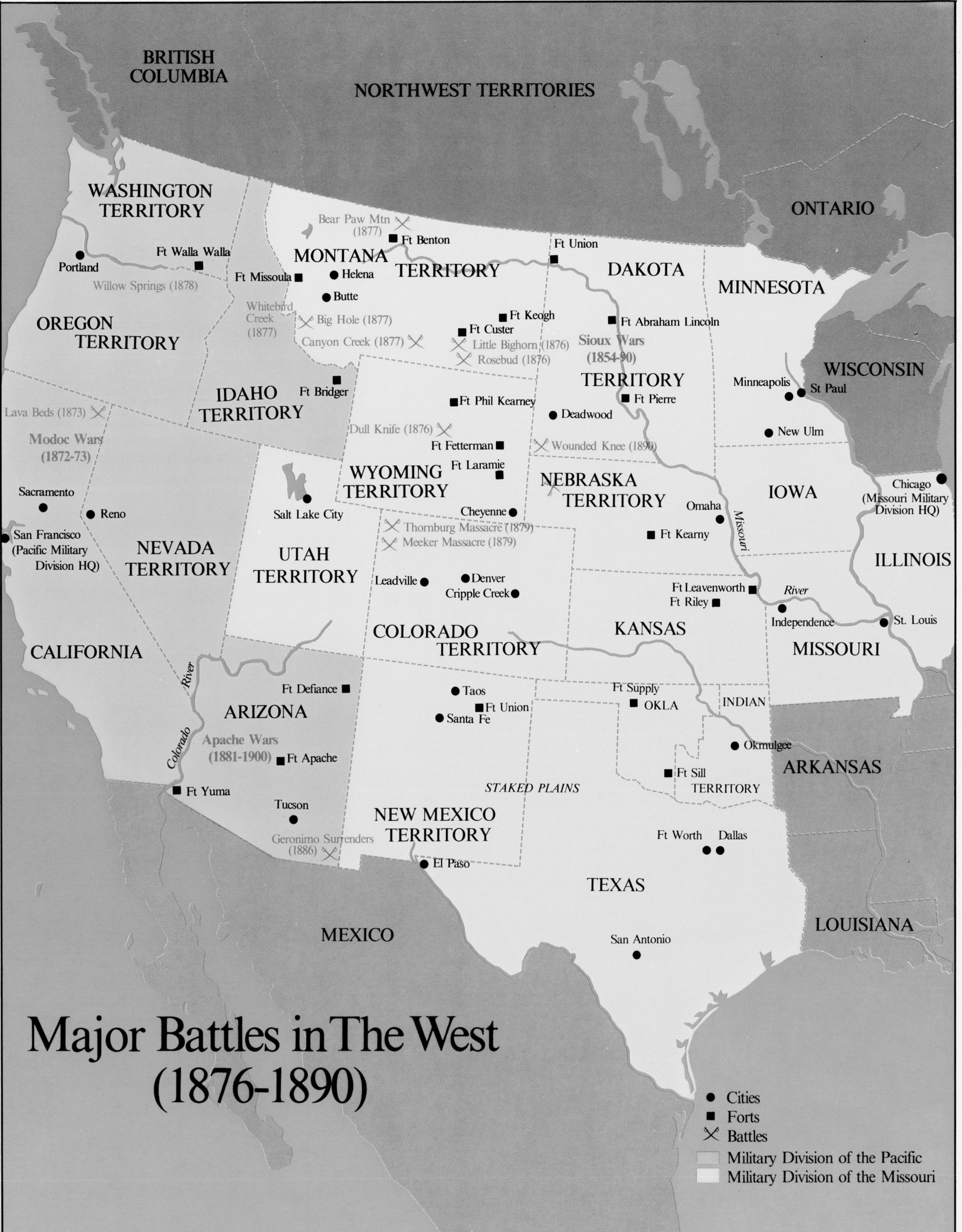
BRITISH COLUMBIA
NORTHWEST TERRITORIES
ONTARIO
WASHINGTON TERRITORY
Portland
Ft Walla Walla
Willow Springs (1878)
OREGON TERRITORY
Lava Beds (1873)
Modoc Wars (1872-73)
Sacramento
Reno
San Francisco (Pacific Military Division HQ)
NEVADA TERRITORY
CALIFORNIA
IDAHO TERRITORY
Ft Missoula
Whitebird Creek (1877)
Ft Bridger
MONTANA TERRITORY
Bear Paw Mtn (1877)
Ft Benton
Helena
Butte
Big Hole (1877)
Canyon Creek (1877)
Ft Keogh
Ft Custer
Little Bighorn (1876)
Rosebud (1876)
Ft Union
DAKOTA TERRITORY
Ft Abraham Lincoln
Sioux Wars (1854-90)
Ft Pierre
Deadwood
Wounded Knee (1890)
MINNESOTA
Minneapolis
St Paul
New Ulm
WISCONSIN
Chicago (Missouri Military Division HQ)
IOWA
ILLINOIS
Ft Phil Kearney
Dull Knife (1876)
Ft Fetterman
Ft Laramie
WYOMING TERRITORY
Cheyenne
Salt Lake City
UTAH TERRITORY
NEBRASKA TERRITORY
Omaha
Ft Kearny
Missouri
Thornburg Massacre (1879)
Meeker Massacre (1879)
Leadville
Denver
Cripple Creek
COLORADO TERRITORY
Ft Leavenworth
Ft Riley
River
Independence
St. Louis
KANSAS
MISSOURI
Colorado River
Ft Defiance
ARIZONA
Apache Wars (1881-1900)
Ft Apache
Ft Yuma
Tucson
Geronimo Surrenders (1886)
Taos
Ft Union
Santa Fe
STAKED PLAINS
NEW MEXICO TERRITORY
El Paso
Ft Supply
OKLA
INDIAN
Okmulgee
Ft Sill
TERRITORY
ARKANSAS
Ft Worth
Dallas
TEXAS
San Antonio
LOUISIANA
MEXICO
Major Battles in The West (1876-1890)
Cities
Forts
Battles
Military Division of the Pacific
Military Division of the Missouri

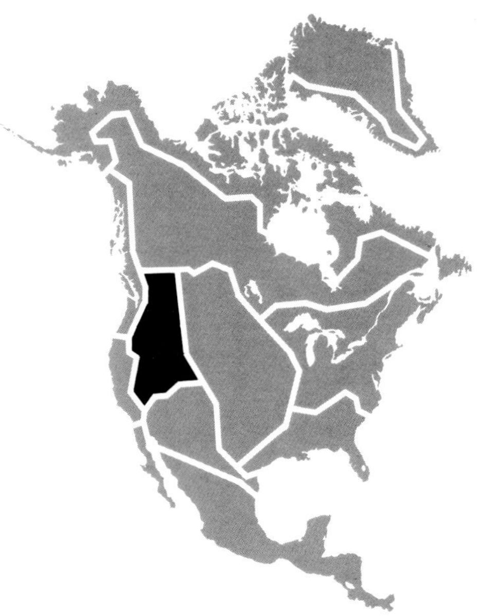

INDIANS OF THE GREAT BASIN

Below: In 1870 William Henry Jackson photographed the camp of Shoshoni Chief Washakie, who was friendly to the whites. The Shoshonis lived in the northeastern part of the Great Basin and were organized in a very loose, unstructured way. During the summer small groups wandered off in search of food and in the winter they settled in small villages. These four-pole skin teepees reflect the influence of the Plains.

Between the Rocky Mountains that divide the continent into the Atlantic and Pacific drainages, and the Sierra Nevada of California and the Cascade range of the Northwest lies a vast basin. Bounded on the south by the Colorado River and Arizona, the Great Basin stretches up through Nevada and Utah to southern Idaho, central Oregon and Washington and on up into British Columbia. The southern part of the Great Basin is a desolate and unforgiving desert, while the northern part, cut by the great river valleys of the Snake, the Columbia and the Fraser, is somewhat more hospitable.

The Indians of the southern part of the Basin, principally the Shoshoni, Paiute, Ute and Bannock, led an extremely difficult existence in which all their activities, like those of the Athabaskans in the far north, were structured around mere subsistence. They were a nomadic people, wandering in the mountains and valleys of the Basin in search of food. Animal life in the area was also sparse. Jackrabbits were the preferred fare. They were not only good to eat but their pelts were used to make clothing. These mammals were not always available, however, and the people of the Basin generally depended on mice and insects, especially locusts, for their protein requirements. Berries and piñon nuts were available but not plentiful. In order to survive in this barren land, its natives had to learn to read and follow the seasons. In the summer, when the blazing sun parched the valley floor and the vegetation became brown and dry, they would climb into the high mountains of the Basin, where it was cooler, where plants still flourished and where an occasional kangaroo rat might be found. In winter, when the snows came to the high country, they would return again to the valley floor. In the northern part of the Basin, life was somewhat easier because of the fertile river

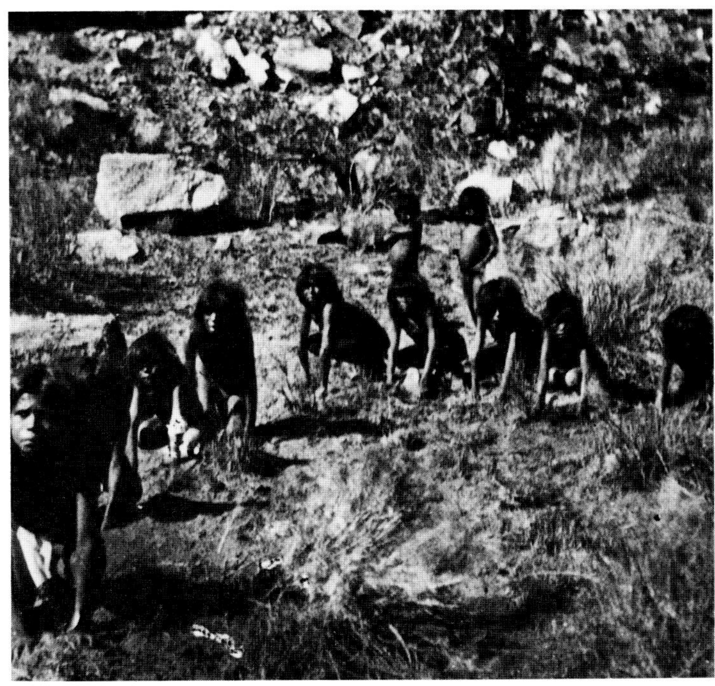

Above: Paiute children in northern Arizona play a game called wolf and deer. During the hot summers they wore little or no clothing.

Next page: The arid Basin is a stark world of rugged beauty.

Left: A Paiute woman in 1872 grinds seeds in the doorway of her brush house. Typical Great Basin homes were temporary, crude and simple structures based on the conical teepee formation.

Above: A Uinta Ute warrior and his bride were photographed in 1874 in northwest Utah. Usually Ute couples lived with or near the bride's family.

Above right: Four Nuaguntit Paiutes gamble in southwest Nevada in 1873.

Above far right: Paiutes used bows and arrows to hunt small game like rabbits and rats. Larger game like deer and antelope were scarce.

valleys. This was also where the Rockies gave way to the lowlands less abruptly, producing the great intermountain country with its rich lakes and forests. This area includes the mountains and valleys of the Idaho Panhandle and British Columbia and the great valleys of western Montana, such as the Bitterroot, the Flathead and the McDonald, lushest of them all.

The Columbia River drainage was the home of a number of important tribes whose names are familiar as important place names to this day, Spokane, Wenatche, Yakima, Umatilla, Klamath, Okanagon and Walla Walla. The Idaho Panhandle was home to the Coeur D'Alene and Nez Percé, while the Kalispell and Flathead lived in the valleys of northwestern Montana.

The peoples of this region, unlike their cousins to the south, developed a rich cultural diversity through interaction with other tribes from the Subarctic, the Northwest Coast, California and the Plains. Unlike any of their neighbors, except the Plains tribes, they became excellent horsemen. Big game in the form of deer and elk were plentiful, as were fish and wild berries and nuts. Trade flourished within the region and with the neighboring regions. Like the Californians but unlike the Indians of the Plains, the people of this area welcomed the white man

Indian Tribes of the Great Basin

Bannock
Cayuse
Coeur d'Alene
Flathead
Gosiute
Kalispell
Klamath
Kootenai
Mono
Nez Percé
Okinagan
Paiute
Palouse
Paviotso
Pend d'Oreille
Shoshoni
Shushwap
Spokane
Thompson
Umatilla
Ute
Walla Walla
Wasco
Washo
Wishram
Yakima

without hostility and generally allowed the white trappers and hunters to share peacefully in the bounty of the land.

Friction evolved, however, as more and more settlers made their way west on the Oregon Trail. In 1847 Dr Marcus Whitman, a fire-and-brimstone missionary, was among 14 whites massacred by Cayuse Indians at his mission near Fort Walla Walla. This led to reprisals against Indians, but the matter did not provoke general hostility the way it might have on the Plains. In the mid-1850s the Rogue River Wars in Oregon renewed the cycle of violence. It took about five difficult years for the Army to put down the rebellious Indians. While the loss of life was not as great as in other Indian wars, the destruction of property was enormous and the wars were costly to both the settlers and to the US government. In 1858, a year after peace came at last to Oregon, the Spokane Wars broke out to the north. The result was a major victory for the US Army and general peace in the whole northwestern United States for the next 20 years.

When war clouds next rolled across the valleys and forests of this land, they would write one of the greatest epics in the history of the Indian Wars and would see the rise to national prominence of one of the greatest Indian leaders of all time. The Nez Percé of the Idaho Panhandle had a record of good relations with their white neighbors, going back to the earlier Indian wars of the region in which they'd remained neutral. The tribe was actually two tribes, an Upper and Lower Nez Percé, with each occupying its own distinct lands but sharing certain common hunting grounds. This distinction, however, was lost on the US government, who in 1863 signed a treaty with the Upper Nez Percé, who in turn signed away the lands of both Nez Percé groups and moved to the Lapwai Reservation. It took over 10 years before white population growth in Lower Nez Percé territory reached a level where it encroached upon the Indians who still were not abiding by the treaty that had been signed for them. Though local white sentiment actually supported creation of a Lower Nez Percé reservation at Wallowa, Congress declined to approve it. Despite the efforts of the diplomatic mission-school-educated Chief Joseph, the southern wing of the tribe was compelled in 1877 to move from the Wallowa Valley onto the Lapwai Reservation, where natural friction developed between the two groups of Indians. Joseph wanted to avoid bloodshed, but members of his Lower Nez Percés went on the warpath, lifting white scalps and bringing the wrath of the US Army. General Oliver Otis Howard and Chief Joseph knew and respected one another but the actions of a few braves had escalated the violence to a point where it couldn't be turned back. Joseph took command and moved his forces to White Bird Canyon, where on 17 June 1877 they defeated the US Army in the first pitched battle of what would be called the Nez Percé War. By the time Howard arrived with more men and heavy artillery, Joseph had moved across the Clearwater River.

It was Chief Joseph's plan to move the tribe north of the Canadian border where the US Army would not follow them, but to do so they would have to get into Montana, cross the Rockies and hundreds of miles of plains. They crossed into Montana near Fort Missoula and managed to either elude or defeat the Army in a series of actions that took them across the Continental Divide and through newly established Yellowstone National Park. As they struck out across the Plains, they were pursued not only by Howard's troopers, but by the Seventh Cavalry under Colonel Nelson "Bearcoat" Miles from Fort Keogh as well. The Nez Percé eluded the Seventh in a skirmish on Canyon Creek and crossed the Missouri at Cow Island on 23

Left, above and right: Flathead Indians parade down Higgins Avenue in Missoula, Montana in August 1955. Missoula is about 50 miles south of the Flathead Reservation. At one time Indians of this region were known for their flat foreheads, developed in infancy after a year of being tied down to a cradleboard.

Below: Nez Percé warriors of the Great Plateau in 1906. The Nez Percé acquired the horse from the Plains, and with their increased mobility they established a widespread and thriving trade. The influence of the Plains is evident in the heavily decorated deerskin clothing, softened hide parfleches (saddlebags) and elaborately beaded shields.

September. A week later the exhausted Nez Percé, still moving their cattle and dependents along with the fighting force, camped in the Bear Paw Mountains. They were finally just about a day's ride from Canada. Howard was still two days behind and Joseph rested easy. Meanwhile, however, Miles managed to get a sizable cavalry force within striking distance. The force took a large number of casualties but managed to surround Joseph almost within sight of Canada. A battle raged for five days, with the Army bringing up Hotchkiss guns to pound the encampment that the cavalry had surrounded. Finally, with no hope left, Joseph surrendered, telling Miles that "from where the sun now stands I will fight no more forever."

A few of the Nez Percé managed to get across the border and link up with Sitting Bull's Sioux, but the bulk of the survivors were sent, not back to Lapwai as promised by Miles, but to a wretched corner of Indian Territory (present-day eastern Oklahoma) instead. In 1885 what was left of the tribe was returned to Lapwai, but Joseph was sent to the Colville Reservation in Washington State where he died on 21 September 1904.

In 1946 a large part of the upper Great Basin, including the Nez Percé country of Idaho, was placed under the jurisdiction of the Portland Area Office of the Bureau of Indian Affairs. In 1967 this office embarked upon a program to strengthen tribal participation in BIA decision making. At first the effort focused on achieving mutual understanding of BIA and tribal decision-making processes through committees, workshops and individual consultation at the agency and area levels. The result was the progressive development of a tribal/BIA working partnership that has evolved into a situation where tribal governments have a key role in recommending, developing and implementing

Far left: A delegation of Flathead Indians congregate with their interpreter in Washington in 1884. The Flatheads were eventually forced into Canada when they could not resist white settlement in Montana.

Above left: Mrs Moses Johnson, an Umatilla woman from Oregon.

Above: Angelic La Moose, granddaughter of a Flathead chief, models an outfit made by her mother at the Flathead Reservation, about 1913.

policy. Between 1976 and 1980 the number of such programs increased from 100 to 275.

In May 1980 Oregon Governor Victor Atiyeh signed an historic executive order restoring criminal jurisdiction over the Umatilla Reservation to the Confederated Tribes of the Umatilla Reservation. This action recognized tribal sovereignty and provided for a judiciary and tribal law enforcement.

In the Portland region of the upper Great Basin are tribal timberlands with the potential to provide a sustained annual harvest of nearly six million board feet of lumber, which translates into 80,000 jobs, many of them held by Indians, and an annual $270 million contribution to the regional economy. The Spokane Reservation has one of the two operating uranium mines in the area, yielding over a million pounds of uranium oxide concentrate annually. Meanwhile, the Nez Percé Reservation contains a major limestone quarry, and the Colville Reservation (to which Chief Joseph was exiled) is the site of a major new copper-molybdenum recovery operation.

Fishing on the great rivers of the Columbia drainage was an important part of Indian culture and economy before the arrival of the white man, and it remains so today, with fishing rights reaffirmed in federal court and upheld by the US Supreme Court. Contemporary Indians fish in the traditional way as well as with sophisticated modern gear.

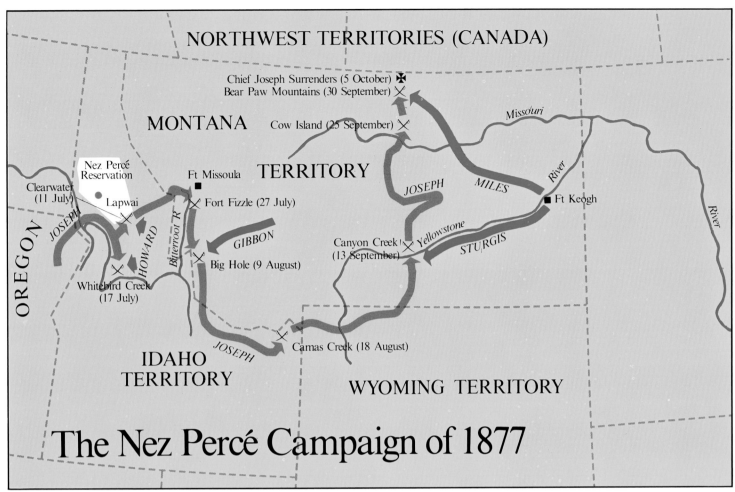

The Nez Percé Campaign of 1877

Left: Chief Joseph (1832–1904) was the great leader of the Nez Percé tribe that occupied the Wallowa Valley of Oregon and Salmon River region of Idaho. The Nez Percé had always avoided fighting with the white man, but in 1877 the government finally provoked warfare when it took possession of Nez Percé land and ordered removal of the tribe to an Idaho reservation. To avoid removal Joseph retreated with his tribe over 1600 miles through Blackfoot territory to Canada, with General Oliver O Howard in pursuit. The Nez Percé War lasted several months, until the tribe was tracked to within 30 miles of the border. It was here that Joseph was forced to surrender on 7 October 1877, when he delivered his most eloquent and remembered words:

> Tell General Howard I know his heart. What he told me before I have in my heart. I am tired of fighting. Our chiefs are killed. Looking Glass is dead. Toohoolhoolzote is dead. The old men are all dead. It is the young men who say yes or no. He who led on the young men is dead. It is cold and we have no blankets. The little children are freezing to death. My people, some of them, have run away to the hills, and have no blankets, no food; no one knows where they are—perhaps freezing to death. I want to have time to look for my children and see how many of them I can find. Maybe I shall find them among the dead. Hear me, my chiefs! I am tired; my heart is sick and sad. From where the sun now stands I will fight no more forever.

The Nez Percé were forced onto a reservation in Indian Territory and not until 1885 were the survivors permitted to return West. However, they were prohibited from resettling in the Wallowa Valley and were moved instead to a reservation in Washington, where Joseph died.

Right: Wolf Necklace was a chief of the Palouse River Indians who lived near the border of Washington and Idaho, adjacent to the Nez Percé lands. This tribe was well known for breeding Appaloosa horses, which were traded with Indians from other regions. These mottled horses were rugged and strong saddle horses. The Nez Percé, however, outdid all other tribes in North America in horsebreeding.

Following page: This Bannock family of sheepeaters was camped near the head of Medicine Lodge Creek, Idaho in 1871. The Bannocks lived in the northern part of the Great Basin, at the edges of the Rocky Mountains, where bighorn sheep were in short supply. The family was the basic unit of their society, and, since the sources of food were in short supply, wandering in a constant search for sustenance was the way of life and the means of survival. Other tribes were organized in larger bands. The Bannocks were also involved in a war with the Army in 1878.

INDIANS OF THE NORTHWEST COAST

West of Seattle and north of Vancouver, stretching up the British Columbia coast through the Alaskan Panhandle, is a remote land of islands and inlets with a coastline longer than the eastern seaboard from Maine to Texas. It is a temperate though fog-shrouded land. It is a mystical land where the clouds swirl close to the heavily wooded hills that rise above the labyrinth of coastal waterways. With the cold moist glove of the ocean fog to the rear, one can stand and look into the warmth of a crackling fire bursting with the wonderful fragrance of big cedar logs and imagine the great culture of the people whose fires once burned on these shores.

Below: Haida totem poles line Old Kasaan village in southeastern Alaska. In the foreground of this photograph are the crests of Chief Skowl, which include the figures of a raven and a grizzly bear. The Haida tribe lived on the Queen Charlotte Islands off the coast of Canada, surrounded by thick woodlands of yellow and red cedar, their most useful resource. With primitive tools they became sophisticated carpenters; to build the longhouses they split the cedar into planks, joining them with tongues and grooves carved into the wood. The completed buildings were enormous—large enough to house as many as 40 people—and they were subdivided into several rooms. Floors were planked and a raised platform was built all around the inside walls. Exterior walls were covered in cedar shingles. At the front of the longhouse reposed the totem pole.

Left: This 13-inch Tlingit shaman's mask, carved from wood and painted blue, red and black, had a hinged flap in the design of a snail. The wooden visage represented one of the shaman's guardian spirits.

Above: A Kwakiutl village as it appeared in 1899, on Hope Island, in the central region of the Northwest Coast.

The Northwest Coast tribes, of whom the major tribes are the Haida, Tlingits, Kwakiutls and Chinook, are descendent from aboriginal people who made their way to the region as early as 8000 BC. The complexity and sophistication of the art and architecture of these people was of a level unequalled by any tribe in North America and matched only by the Mayas and Aztecs in Mesoamerica. They lived in elaborate log houses, constructed of massive cedar planks without the use of iron tools. They plied the waterways of the region in huge, elaborately carved, 65-foot dugout boats. Their decorative art, chiefly textiles and carving, was on a par with much of what was being done in China or Europe.

The most outstanding manifestations of their carving were the huge totem poles, which were proudly displayed next to nearly every house and which to this day exist in the Indian villages of the Northwest Coast. The early missionaries to the region were horrified by the totem poles, believing them to be designed to pay tribute to the horrible heathen gods worshipped by these misguided savages. It was, however, the missionaries who were misguided. The totem poles were entirely secular, the equivalent of a European crest or coat of arms. In the same way that a German family might select a rampant lion or an eagle to symbolize its view of itself, a Tlingit family or clan might select a bear or a raven as its "totem" animal. Totem poles could contain a whole pantheon of animals representing a legend surrounding that animal, possibly including the huge thunderbird, who lived high in the mountains and who created thunderstorms by flapping its wings. The great height of the totem poles was controlled only by the length of the big cedar logs from which they were carved, and they frequently reached in excess of 50 feet.

The totem poles feature prominently in our view of Northwest Coast decorative art, partly because of their size but also because the sunlight and open air has helped preserve them. Much of the other work carved from the soft cedar has decayed over time and been lost. Few

Indian Tribes of the Northwest Coast

Alsea	**Cowichan**	**Makah**	**Squamish**
Bella Bella	**Cowlitz**	**Nisquali**	**Takelma**
Bella Coola	**Haida**	**Nootka**	**Tenino**
Chastacosta	**Kalapuya**	**Puyallup**	**Tillamook**
Chehalis	**Klallam**	**Quileute**	**Tlingit**
Chimakuan	**Klamath**	**Quinault**	**Tsimshian**
Chinnesyan	**Klikitat**	**Siuslaw**	**Twana**
Chinook	**Kusa**	**Skagit**	**Umpqua**
Comox	**Kwakiutl**	**Snoqualmi**	**Yaquina**
Coos	**Lummi**	**Songish**	

Above: Based on their journal writings, Charles Russell painted Meriwether Lewis's and William Clark's encounter with Chinook Indians in 1805 on the lower Columbia River. The Shoshoni woman, Sacagawea, served as guide and interpreter of sign language for the two explorers as they carried out their peaceful mission. This meeting was one of the first encounters between the Northwest tribes and the white man. The elaborately carved canoes of the Chinooks were constructed without nails or metal parts of any kind, yet they rivalled those of Lewis and Clark in both size and sophistication.

Above: A Kwakiutl village on Hope Island in the Queen Charlotte Straits at the turn of the century. The Northwestern Indians evolved a dramatic, distinctive and enormous art form that became their trademark and is still created today. The Haida tribe were especially skilled at carving the large wooden totem poles. These massive sculptures, carved from giant cedar logs, are the coats of arms or family trees that identify a family's ancestry. Many are brightly colored and reach as high as 30 feet. Totem poles are a bold and proud display of the identity of the inhabitants of a house. Clans named themselves after animals from their mythology who had performed heroic feats, and artists devised stylized symbolic figures to represent each creature, highlighting certain of the features. No other clan was permitted to use those symbols. Compared to the northern Haida, the Kwakiutl Indians tended to use forms directly from nature. They achieved a more three-dimensional effect by carving more deeply into the wood and by attaching wings, horns or plumes to the structure. Totem poles had no religious significance, contrary to the common belief held by outsiders. Similar poles were carved as built-in supports for a house; others served as poles to hold the ashen remains of a cremated body or as a grave marker for a dead shaman. The shaman was the only member of Northwestern Indian society to be buried; all other bodies were cremated.

Right: Two Tlingit girls, Tsacotna and Natsanitna, from Cooper River in Alaska, pose for a photograph in 1903 and show off their decorated clothing and jewelry. Tlingits were avid traders and bargained for brass buttons that they turned into nose rings. In later years, mother of pearl buttons became available and were applied to clothing and blankets as trimming. Buttons and dentalium jewelry were symbols of status among Northwestern tribes. In the past when young girls like these reached a marriageable age, they wore a labret or plug in the lower lip and the family tattoo on the outside of their hand.

Northwest Coast artifacts predate the nineteenth century. Because separate cultures in other regions had earlier contact with white men and produced stone and metal artifacts, our knowledge of them goes back further.

It is ironic that this great culture was one of the last to be contacted by Europeans. The East Coast was fully settled, Quebec, Boston and New York were thriving cities and the great cultures of Mesoamerica had been pretty well wiped out by the time the first contact was made in the Northwest. Benjamin Franklin was a prominent Philadelphia printer and had perfected his Franklin stove by 1741 when the great Danish explorer Vitus Bering first encountered the Tlingits during one of his voyages on behalf of the Russian tsar. It was not until 1778 that British Captain James Cook actually traded with the Northwest Coast people. By the time Meriwether Lewis and William Clark arrived in Chinook country at the mouth of the Columbia, the total interaction with Europeans was minimal.

The Northwest Coast tribes, particularly the Tlingits, were consummate traders. These tribes traded both among themselves and with the tribes on the other side of the coastal mountain ranges. Trading became highly developed because, unlike the tribes in other regions, subsistence took

1903.
Bros. # 872.

Left: A totem pole from the Provincial Museum in Victoria, British Columbia. Many of the wooden artifacts of the Northwest have been destroyed over the years, either by man or the elements.

Right: This Chilkat dress is a museum piece that was woven from a yarn mixture of cedar-bark fiber and mountain goat wool. Equal portions were dyed blue, yellow and black or left natural white. The weaving process, when done by traditional methods, was extremely time consuming. A wealthy father or husband commissioned his daughter or wife to make him a garment according to the design he provided, a symmetrical arrangement of figures often derived from the clan symbols. The completed garment, or blanket, was highly valued. It was a sign of great wealth and was usually passed down to other members of the family.

Below: The Northwestern Indians carved colorful hinged masks to represent particular spirits in ceremonies. Only the owner knew the story that inspired its creation and its true meaning.

Bottom: The interior of Tlingit chief Clart-Reech's house, *c.* 1895.

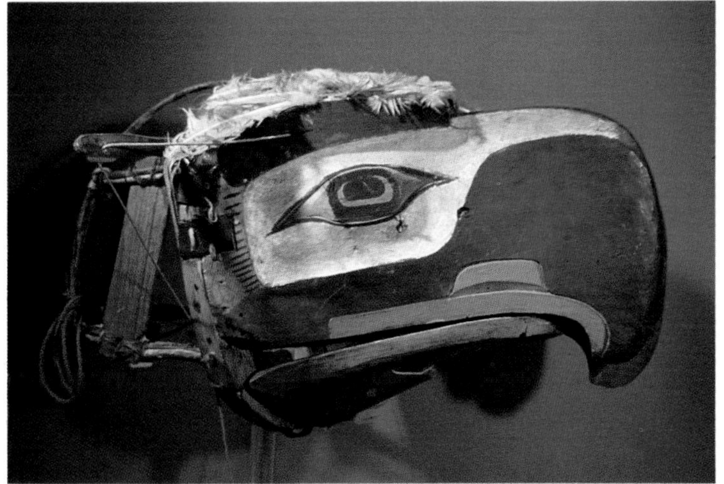

Above: A simple Northwest Coast carved bear mask.

Right: Masked Kwakiutl Shaman Society dancers assemble for the Hamatsa Dance, *c.* 1915. The highest ranking member is the Hamatsa, or Cannibal Dancer (rear left). The remaining dancers represent other evil spirits.

Next page: This nearly 5-foot long mask represents the Raven. The Raven eats the eyes of the Cannibal Dancer's victims in the Hamatsa dance.

such a small part of their time. The salmon ran in abundance in the summer and formed the staple in the Northwest Coast diet. Enough of them could be gathered in the summer to last the entire year, and much free time ensued. Accumulation of wealth as well as artistic pursuits became a primary preoccupation throughout most of the year. Wealth was measured in both material goods and in slaves, the latter being captured farther south among the more docile California tribes. Rank within a tribe was based on wealth rather than hereditary, so a low-born person could acquire high rank through accumulation of wealth and status. Although religion was not important among the materialistic tribes of the area, shamans did exist, and many became extremely wealthy themselves through the fees they charged for their unique services.

The centerpiece of the Northwest Coast cultural life was the great ceremony called the potlatch. This ceremony was a manifestation of the obsession with wealth and consisted of an enormous party thrown in celebration of the host's wealth. Hundreds of guests would be invited, frequently from two or more clans. The guests would arrive in their best warships, dressed in their best costumes, ready for up to 10 days of feasting and general merriment. There would be singing and dancing, and toasting of the host and his clan. Rituals were performed and all the guests ate to the point of bursting. For the host, however, the potlatch was

(Text continues on page 157)

Below: A gable-roofed house and totem pole of a Bella Coola village in British Columbia, pre-1901. In the Northwest houses were built under the supervision of an expert carpenter and skilled craftsmen were hired to carve the totem poles for the front of the house.

Left: A shaman probably used a tool like this 7-inch bone soul catcher during curing rituals to suck out the cause of the disease.

Lower left: This elaborately carved duck-shaped rattle belonged to a Tlingit shaman. The shaman, either a male or a female, dressed in a carved mask and blanket for a ritual cure, shaking the rattle and singing in the effort to learn from the spirits the cause of the illness. The shaman never cut or groomed his or her hair and was a fearful sight during ceremonies.

Next page, left: Kwakiutl carved masks used for storytelling ceremonies were often of two parts. The exterior mask was attached with hinges and was opened at the appropriate moment to reveal an interior mask.

Next page, right: No two shamans' masks were the same. These Indians respected individual creativity, and that included the shaman's.

Top left: A boatload of Makah men bring a whale ashore at Neah Bay, Washington, *c.* 1926. The sealskin buoys kept the whale afloat.

Far left: A Quinaielt Indian holds a dog salmon in Washington in 1936. Regular annual salmon catches provided great wealth in the Northwest.

Left: A button blanket indicates the status of Hamasoka, principal chief of a Kwakiutl village. Mother of pearl buttons were obtained through trade and attached to blankets for decoration.

Above: At the end of a Kwakiutl potlach in 1901 the guests leave with extravagant gifts. In an ostentatious display of wealth, the more affluent hosts destroyed their own belongings by tossing them into the sea or, as the wafts of cedar smoke testify in this case, by burning them.

a serious event. It was a manifestation of his wealth that he could afford to repeat only a few times (if any) in his lifetime, and for which he would prepare for up to a year. In order to demonstrate his great wealth, he would give it away, the theory being that it was so vast that he could not only throw this huge party, he could send his guests away in boats loaded to the gunwales with valuable gifts. Some potlatch hosts were recorded to have given away thousands of elaborately woven blankets. A man might nearly bankrupt himself throwing his potlatch, but he would gain much prestige and would soon, of course, certainly be invited to his neighbor's potlatch, where he would himself receive an enormous pile of gifts. With the rapid influx of white traders in the latter part of the nineteenth century, the character of the potlatch changed. Mass-produced blankets took the place of those that took months of handwork apiece to complete. Worst of all, the white man began to take a dim view of the potlatch. From 1884 until 1951, when all mention of it was striken from the books, the potlatch was illegal in Canada.

Today the Indians of the Northwest Coast set out after the salmon, not in elaborately carved dugouts, but in gasoline-powered fishing boats. Competition with white fishermen is serious now and the salmon don't run like they did in earlier days. Roads have come to some, but not all, of the villages, and the totem poles are still there. The blankets are being made by hand again but there are fewer of them. Today, when the clouds descend to the tops of the hills still clad in a thick mantle of tall cedar, and the water on the inlet becomes quiet, one can almost hear the chant of the Kwakiutl shaman above the crackling of the fragrant campfire on the beach.

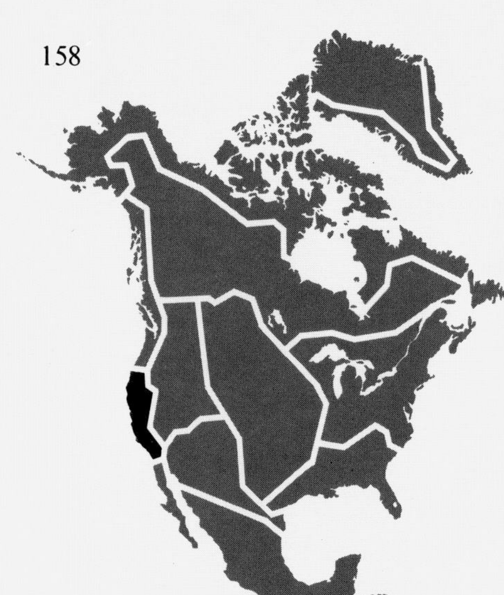

INDIANS OF CALIFORNIA

Below: Laura Somersal, a Pomo-Wapo, teaches a Native American Studies class at Sonoma State College the traditional art of basketmaking. The nonagenarian is an acclaimed living legend and is one of the foremost Indian basketmakers of her time.

Below right: A high quality of workmanship prevailed among California's basketmakers, especially among the Pomos. Although other materials were widely available, Pomos used mainly willow, sedge root, bullrush root and redbud bark, which they wove into numerous designs by a combination of methods. The four feather and shell gift boxes at the front left are fine examples of their decorative skills. These boxes are highly prized and greatly admired by Indians and whites alike.

The State of California has always represented a sort of land at the end of the rainbow to the rest of the United States. For the prospectors of 1849 it was the gold rush and the dream of great wealth that actually came true for many. For midwestern farmers in the 1930s it was an escape from the Dust Bowl in the rich farmland of the central valley. For the baby boom youth of the 1960s it was the lure of the Jefferson Airplane and the exotic culture of the Haight Ashbury. For several generations past and present it was and is the unreal glamour of Hollywood and the magnificent cosmopolitan charm of San Francisco.

For the native peoples of California, too, this place was a Garden of Eden. The area south of the Siskiyou Mountains near the present-day Oregon border, west of the Cascades near the present Nevada border, and north of the Mojave

Desert that stretches from southern California into Arizona and northern Mexico is a temperate land. It is blessed with good soil and sufficient rainfall. The weather is generally good. It was this land that a polyglot of diverse peoples migrated many centuries ago.

A large population developed here but, because of the many incompatible languages, there was little interaction. Since food supplies were relatively abundant, little in the way of warfare took place. There were feuds but little of the type of warring that took place on the Plains, for example. The dwellings were simple and the lifestyle rather easy-going. Because they became rather docile, California Indians were easy marks when the Northwest tribes came south in search of slaves.

The major tribes in northern California, the Pomos, Yuroks, Hupas and Miwoks, subsisted on acorns, berries, wild game and fish plucked from streams. The Chumash of southern California used 25-foot canoes to seek out a supply of ocean fish so important in their diet. The Indians of California developed no towns and cities like their neighbors in the Northwest and Southwest, and their ceremonial life was, as near as can be ascertained, of a smaller scale than that in any part of the continent except the Great Basin.

These people encountered the white man in the form of the Spanish conquistadores and later Spanish missionaries, who transplanted a good deal of their culture and religion

Above: Contemporary Pomo children play a ball game on Rattlesnake Island. Pomos enjoyed active ball games like lacrosse and soccer. Games were played all over North America for entertainment, as a means of developing certain skills or for earning honors. Quiet games played with dice and counters were often reserved for women. Men enjoyed playing a guessing game with opponents who had to guess which hand held certain marked objects. Gambling was the natural accompaniment to all games.

Below: Each medicine man carried his own personal bundle of possessions that he used to cure disease. It was usually passed on to him by the shaman who tutored him or the society in which he learned his trade. The items that make up this bundle belonged to Thomas Smith, a Miwok singing doctor from Bodega Bay in northern California. Included are the animal skin he wore during the curing ritual, a cane whistle, pouches for carrying herbs, mortar and pestles for mixing medicines, obsidian knife blades, feathers, an embroidered moccasin paint bag and a rattle.

in this new land. The first of a chain of missions was established at San Diego in 1769 and by 1776 they ranged up the coast (a day's ride apart) to San Francisco. In contrast to the more warlike tribes of the Plains and elsewhere, many of California's Indians willingly became "mission Indians," working at the missions and gradually adopting the more elaborate Hispanic culture. The result was that by the time Spanish rule ended in the 1820s, the Indian population had been decimated by European diseases and its cultures lost. After a period as a semi-autonomous province of Mexico, California became more

Above: Members of the Hupa tribe from Humboldt County, California assemble for the White Deerskin Dance in the 1890s. This festive dance was one of two that made up the second part of the World Renewal ceremony and followed the sacred ritual. The Hupa chiefs in the foreground carry the sacred obsidian knive and wear headdresses made of sea lion teeth. The longer teeth were of greater value.

Dancers wore outfits provided by wealthy members of the tribe; the more elaborate costumes indicated the affluence and community status of the individual donor. Costumes were made of deerskin or civet cat skin. The dancers, bedecked in shell necklaces and feathered headdresses covering their eyes, carried poles brandishing the full skins of deer, complete with stuffed heads and legs still attached.

Albino deerskins like the ones here shown were the most valuable kind and ownership of them indicated high social status.

Indian Tribes of California

Chumash
Costanoan
Fernandeno
Gabrielino
Hupa
Karok
Luiseno
Maidu
Miwok
Modoc
Pit River
Pomo
Salina
Shasta
Tipai
Wappo
Wintun
Wiyot
Yana
Yokuts
Yuki
Yurok

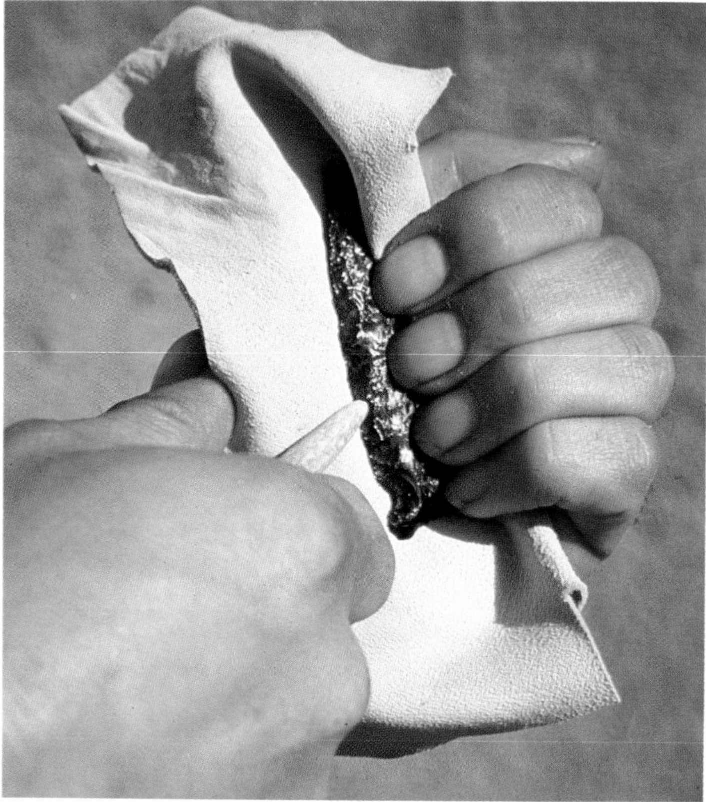

and more Americanized and in 1850 a state of the Union. During this time, the Indians, demoralized after the end of Spanish rule, with no culture of their own to fall back on, became more and more like the Mexicans and Americans, intermarrying with them and adopting their names. By 1860, when the Sioux, the Cheyenne and the Apaches still dominated the Plains and Southwest, Indian culture in California had all but vanished.

It would be untrue to say that there were no conflicts between Indians and whites in California, but those that did take place were between handfuls of combatants on either side and they rose up over isolated incidents much as they would between two groups of whites. There was no large-scale warfare—none, that is, until the Modoc War of 1872–73. The Modocs were a small tribe living in northeastern California on the fringe of the northern edge of the Great Basin. The Modocs were related to the Klamaths of Oregon and it was to the Klamath reservation that they were assigned when their land was ceded to the US government in 1864. Bad feelings between whites and Modocs were deeper than between whites and any other California tribes, dating back to the 1852 massacre of 75 whites at Tule Lake. Ben Wright of Yreka put together a vigilante posse and lured 46 prominent Modocs to a proposed peace talk that resulted in the death of 41 of them. Wright was rewarded with the

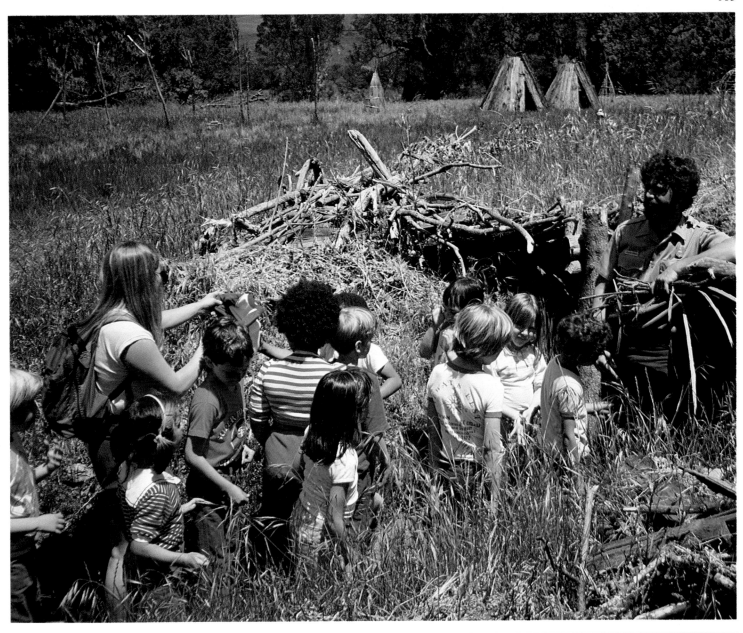

Above left: The Spanish priests established their first mission in southern California in San Diego in 1769 and followed it with several others, including this one at Santa Barbara, all built for the purpose of Christianizing Indians. The Indians welcomed the missionaries, who also tried to be their protectors, but in the process of becoming "mission Indians" they lost their cultural ways. The Spanish were far more successful than the English at missionary work, and they converted large numbers of Indians in a short period of time.

Left: Flaking obsidian gave the stone an extremely sharp edge that was ideal for tools and weapons.

Above: Children of the Pacific Primary kindergarten in San Francisco visit a reconstructed coast Miwok village at Point Reyes National Seashore in California. The buildings being reconstructed are accurate replicas of those that would have appeared in an Indian village in this area a century ago. The village is being rebuilt by volunteers, using the same types of tools, materials and methods used by the Miwoks. In the background are the crude conical bark houses and the open framework of a Miwok-style acorn grainery. Brush or bark were placed over the teepee-type arrangement of poles and tied down with vine. Miwoks also lived in simple lean-tos as well as in underground dwellings. Most California Indians lived in small villages and the family was the basic unit of society. The ranger stands at the tunnel entrance to the earth-covered subterranean sweathouse. The circular sweathouse was the place where all ceremonies were held and the place where adult males of the village slept. Groups of Indians gathered on a daily basis to sweat, an exercise they regarded as a pleasant pastime. In California Indians built a large fire to stimulate sweating; in the Northeast and in other regions, water was poured over hot stones to produce steam and thereby cause sweating.

Right: The Pomo Big Head dancer participated in a variety of ceremonies and was usually the member of a secret society. The identity of the dancer was disguised by the enormous headdress made of grasses and feathers atop painted willow rods that covered the entire face.

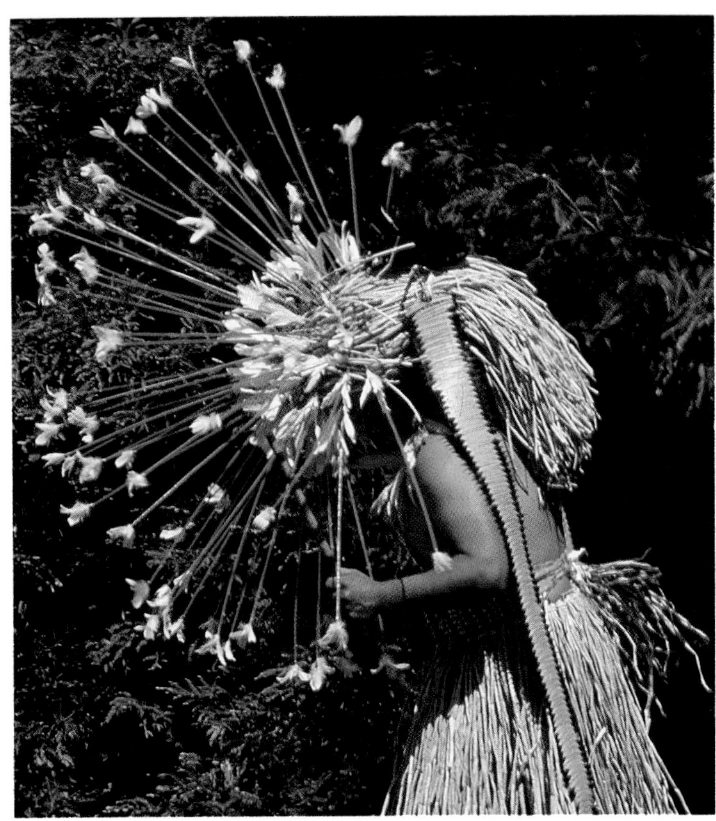

Above: Umits, a Yurok Indian, raises a dip net used for catching fish at the beginning of the century. Nets were made out of sea grass and weighed down with stones.

Left: A Yurok woman wears a traditional full-length shell skirt. The dentalium shells, sometimes used as money, were worn as a sign of wealth.

Above right: Pomo men from the Garcia River, dressed for a baseball game, were photographed on 4 July 1906.

Right: Scarfaced Charley was a member of Captain Jack's band and became leader of the Modocs on the Quapaw Reservation in Indian Territory.

Far right: Captain Jack, Chief of the Modocs, tried to keep peace when his tribe refused to live on a reservation but was forced into war with the Army in 1872. During one battle he killed a US general and was betrayed by his own men. He was hanged in 1873.

post of Indian agent and the bad feelings became engrained on both sides as a result. Shortly after the signing of the 1864 treaty, a large number of Modocs under Kientepoos (Captain Jack) left the reservation for their former home, remaining there for five years before briefly returning to the reservation in 1869. Trouble between the Klamaths and Modocs ensued, and Captain Jack once again led his people back to the old Modoc country on California's Lost River. Here they refused a 26 November 1872 government order to return to the reservation. The US Army was ordered to use a show of force to compel their obedience. On 29 November about 30 troopers made contact with the Modocs and most of the latter put down their weapons peaceably. Scarfaced Charlie was a bit reluctant to do so, and when an officer attempted to force him it proved a fatal mistake. The ensuing firefight developed into what would become known as the Modoc War, or the Lava Beds Campaign, after the

Above three: This young Apache woman performs a traditional blessing with herb incense on the last remaining grounds of the aboriginal Pomos, where the land is going under as a result of the construction of the Warm Springs Dam. The herbs are then passed over the area blessed. Dam construction has resulted in the inundation of much Indian land across the United States.

The Indians have, however, benefitted from the whites in at least one way. English now serves as a common language among most and ties between tribes have been forged that never could have existed before. Indians throughout North America suffered from disunity because of their numerous languages, and this was a major weakness in their effort to halt the loss of their land to early white settlement.

volcanic badlands into which Captain Jack and his approximately 80 warriors withdrew.

By spring they were surrounded and a meeting was set up in an attempt to negotiate a peaceful conclusion to the affair. A disagreement ensued in which General E R S Canby fell victim to a bullet from Captain Jack's gun and in which Bogus Charlie killed Dr Eleazer Thomas as he was attempting to escape, having been wounded by another Modoc, Boston Charlie. Within moments, other troopers reached the council tent only to find the two men dead, another wounded and the Indians gone. In their attempts to catch the Indians in the labyrinth that was the Lava Beds, the Army took heavy casualties during the ensuing weeks. Over time, discord developed in the Modoc camp and caused some of the Indians, including Bogus Charlie, to turn sides. After having been surrounded twice and having lost many of his best men to Army bullets or desertion, Captain Jack surrendered. Six Modocs were arraigned for murder and four, including Jack, were hanged at Fort Klamath on 3 October 1873 in front of 500 Klamath Indians. The remainder of the Modoc tribe, then numbering 247 and including Bogus Charlie, were sent to a tiny plot of land in Indian Territory (now eastern Oklahoma), and a few of the very worst offenders were sent to Fort Marion, Florida, where it is reported that they converted to Christianity.

California's only major Indian war took fewer than a hundred lives, involved Indians which could more accurately be included among Great Basin tribes and occurred long after nearly all of the California tribes had been assimilated into mainstream white culture. However, California was yet to be the setting of a really important milestone in the Indian's long history of confrontation with the white man. On 8 March 1964, just over 90 years after Captain Jack left the state for the last time and after Hollywood had been making movies about the Old West for longer than the Old West actually lasted, five Indians climbed out of a boat onto Alcatraz Island in San Francisco Bay. These five, under the leadership of 42-year-old Allen Cottier, a Sioux, were there to occupy the abandoned federal prison under the provisions of a century-old treaty allowing Indians the use of unused government land. The occupation was short-lived, but it was repeated on 20 November 1969 when a 27-year-old Mohawk named Richard Oakes led another occupation force onto the island. This time they were followed by hundreds of Indians from around the country who took occupation as a symbol of past broken treaties and increasing Indian militancy. The government branded the takeover illegal but took a hands-off attitude while the local papers made light of the situation and the occupiers made plans for a cultural center or even an Indian university on the island. At one point the number of Indians on Alcatraz may have numbered in the thousands but by the summer of 1971, when federal marshals arrived to retake the island, only 15 remained.

Today, California has a greater number of Indians than any other state, though most of them, like many of the rest of California's population, are immigrants from other states, other tribes. Of the Indians now living in California, just over half live in the state's urban areas, where unemployment is higher than for any other minority group. For them it is the cultural shock of leaving the extremely rural atmosphere of reservation life for the urban centers of America's most populous state.

Previous page: The annual late-summer Sacramento Pow Wow is extremely popular and attracts thousands of Indians from all over the United States. They get together to perform, compete and exhibit and sell native crafts.

Above left: Pomo men and women prepare for a dance in 1928. Like most California tribes, the Pomo celebrated a number of events with ritual dancing, including the acorn harvest, salmon catches, secret society events and a female's entry into puberty. Young men were initiated into manhood during the Ghost and Kuksu ceremonies, out of the presence of women.

Far left: A Yuki Indian from Mendocino County in 1900 wears a large feather headdress of magpie feathers and yellowhammer quill bands to partially disguise his face. This is the dance costume of a Kuksu secret society member who represents one of the various spirits during the Hesi ceremonial dance. This person plays the role of Chelitu in the three-person dance, and he directs the movements of his partner, the Big Head dancer Tuya, while the chorus chants and two drummers beat their drums. Moki, the supreme spirit, leads the dance.

Left: Pomo boys play typical Indian stick games similar to a game of heads or tails. The rounded sides of the sticks are marked and the flat sides are blank. Players toss six sticks in the air and keep score according to what lands face up. Indians were dedicated gamblers and gambling often went hand in hand with any type of game.

Above: Wintun Joe and his wife were photographed at McCloud Reservation near Redding in northern California in 1903. According to the locals on the reservation, he was given Thomas as a last name by the whites after he uttered the Wintu word "tome," meaning to tell the truth, when questioned about a robbery at Old Shasta.

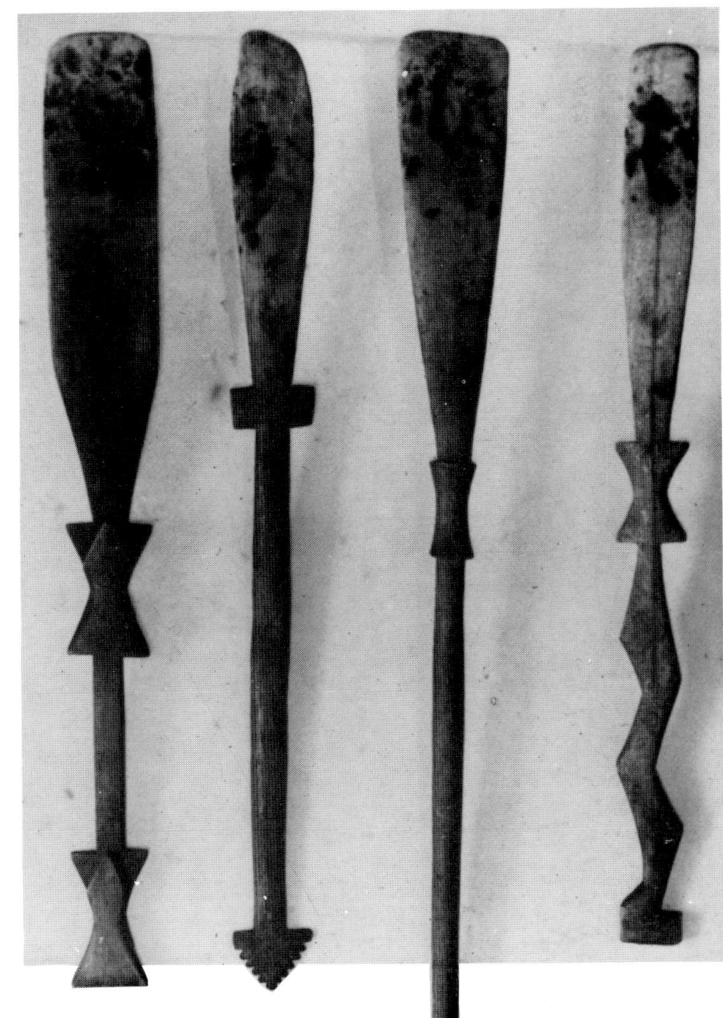

Right: Flattened paddles were used by California Indian women to make acorn mush. Oak trees were plentiful in the interior regions and the acorn was a staple part of most California Indian diets.

The nut was cracked with a stone, ground into flour with a mortar and pestle and then soaked or washed a number of times to remove the bitter tannic acid. The acorn meal was then digestible and could be boiled to make mush or baked into a flat bread. Acorns were harvested in the fall and stored in graineries outdoors. Inland Indians traded acorns with coastal Indians in return for fish.

Native American Population by State 1890

(Twenty most populous states.) US total=249,273*

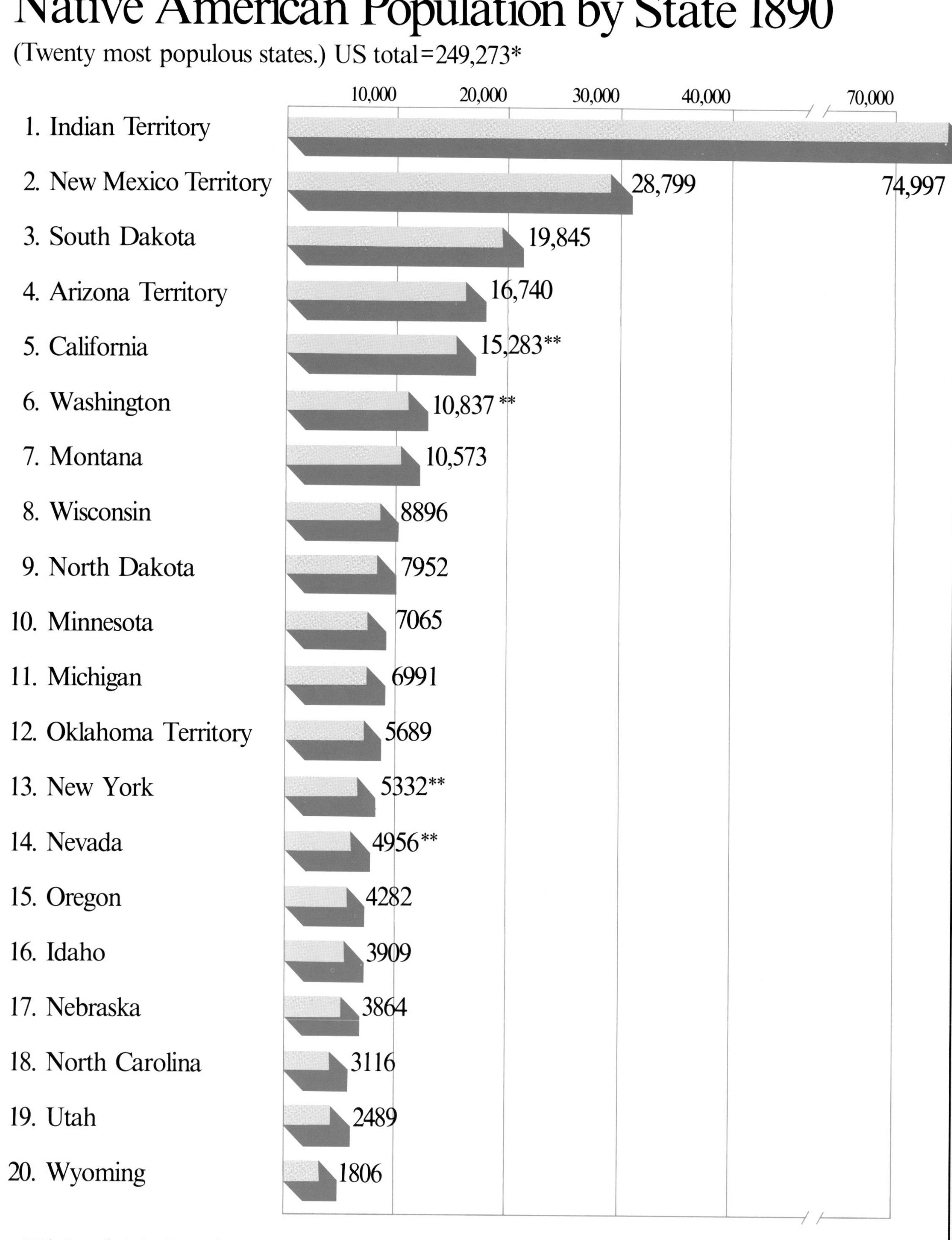

*This figure includes 568 Native Americans listed as War Department prisoners.

**In all of the states listed, much less than a quarter of the Native American population lived off the reservations, with the exception of Washington, where 27% lived off-reservation, California (67%), Nevada (69%) and New York (100%).

Native American Population by State 1990

(Twenty most populous states.) US total=1,959,234

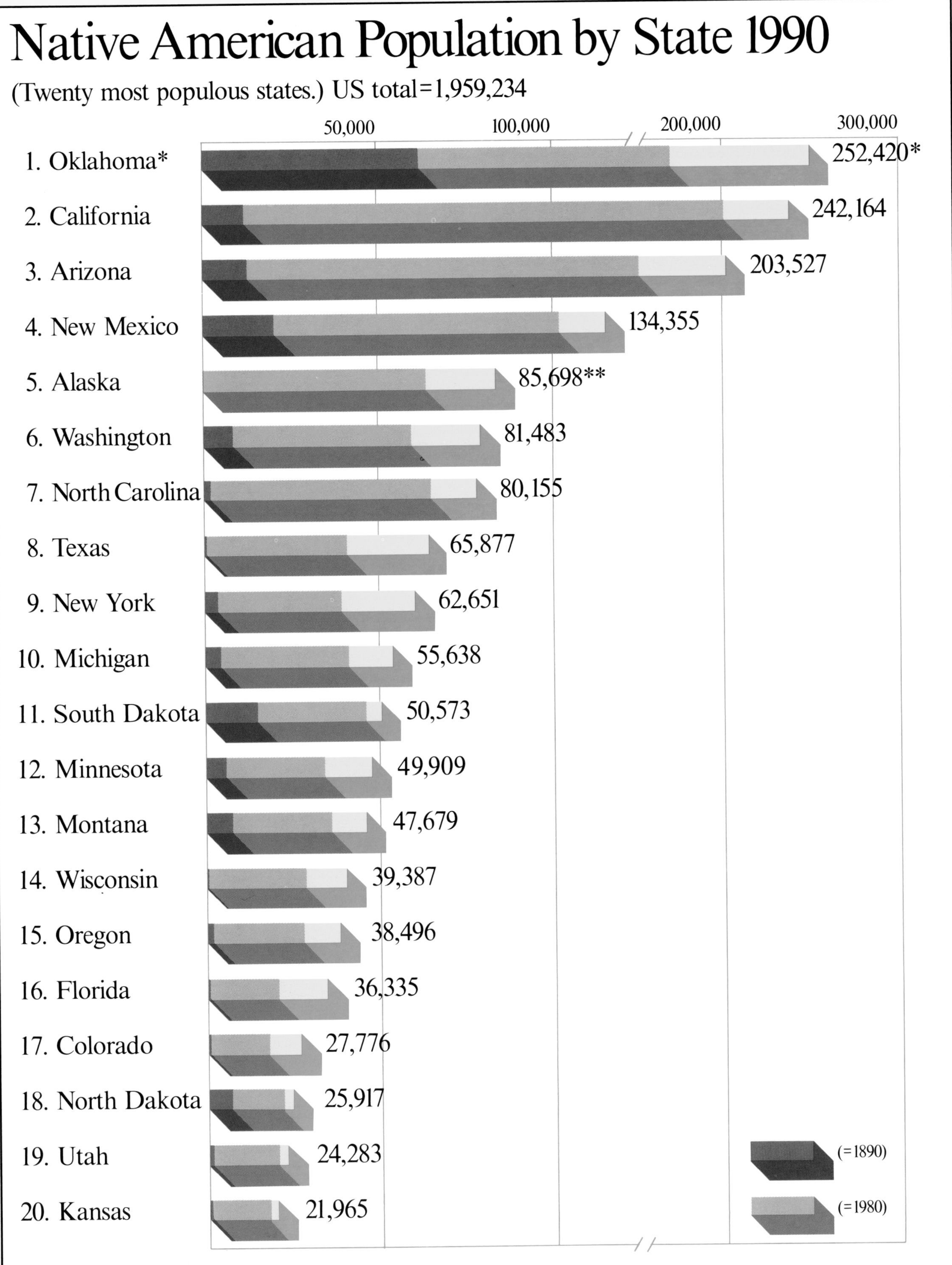

*The State of Oklahoma, created in 1907, constituted a merger of the former Oklahoma Territory and Indian Territory.

**The Native American population of Alaska was not counted in 1890.

INDIANS OF THE SOUTHWEST

Below: This was the way the Laguna Pueblo appeared in 1879. Indians of the Southwest lived in sun-dried mud brick apartment-style buildings in villages called pueblos. The pueblo dwellers were the ancestors of the ancient Anasazi who developed one of the great civilizations of the Southwest and lived in caves on cliff sides.

Inset: A young Laguna Pueblo girl from New Mexico holds a child. The Pueblos surpassed all Indians in their skills with pottery, and it was the women who created these masterpieces. Geometric designs prevailed but as more colors became available, naturalistic forms became common, such as the stylized bird often seen on Acoma pottery. In spite of borrowed features, each tribe evolved its own distinct style and designs. Unfortunately Laguna pottery is rarely seen outside of the pueblo.

In the forests and canyons of the present-day states of Arizona and New Mexico amid the spectacular red sandstone mesas, there arose one of the most complex of prehistoric North American cultures. Preserved for posterity by the dry air of the high desert are the remains of the settlements of the Anasazi people. They built cities with multistory apartment houses, such as the ones extant at Canyon de Chelly, Arizona, developed farming and flourished peacefully between roughly 700 AD and 1100 AD. Their culture was evidently based on a delicate climatic balance which apparently collapsed in a period of severe droughts and/or natural disasters that continued until about 1350, by which time the Anasazi had disappeared and their place taken by the tribes that inhabit this land today. In the northwest corner of New Mexico and in the northeast corner of Arizona, respectively, live the Zuñi and Hopi, nicknamed Pueblos by the Spaniards, who live in adobe cities similar to those of the Anasazi. Throughout the same area, but spreading even further and surrounding the areas of the Pueblos, live the Athabaskan-speaking Navajo. Across the central and southern parts of Arizona and New Mexico, extending into part of Texas and northern Mexico, are the various Athabaskan-speaking Apache tribes. The Pueblo Indians, principally the Hopi and Zuñi with their unique languages, have been there for longer than the Athabaskan speakers. In fact, the Hopi have been in place for about as long as any tribe in the United States. The Indians in the pueblos have been farmers for centuries, raising corn, beans, squash and tobacco on family plots around the pueblos. Deer and rabbits were hunted for meat and their skins used to make clothing. Everything, right down to the seeds for the spring planting, was owned by the women. Descent was reckoned through the mother's side of the family. A Pueblo male would be a member of his mother's clan, making his sister's children part of his clan, but his own children part of his wife's clan. A man's role traditionally was to hunt, and also to regulate the religious life of the tribe. Men organized the rituals and celebrations and impersonated the Kachinas in the elaborate coming-of-age rituals inflicted upon pubescent children. Kachinas were spirits associated with the annual cycle of birth, death and rebirth that lived underground from October through April and moved among the people the rest of the year.

Above: A man and woman of Laguna Pueblo, New Mexico wear cloth garments typical of the Southwest. The woman's dress was always tied over the right shoulder. Both wore hardsoled buckskin moccasins. Many present-day Lagunas wear these on occasion.

Below: Present-day Laguna Pueblo looks similar to the village of a hundred years ago. Southwest Indians resisted vigorous Spanish efforts to convert them and were slow to accept Christianity. As the white cross indicates, some Indians converted over the years, while others adopted aspects of Christianity and blended them into a new native religion.

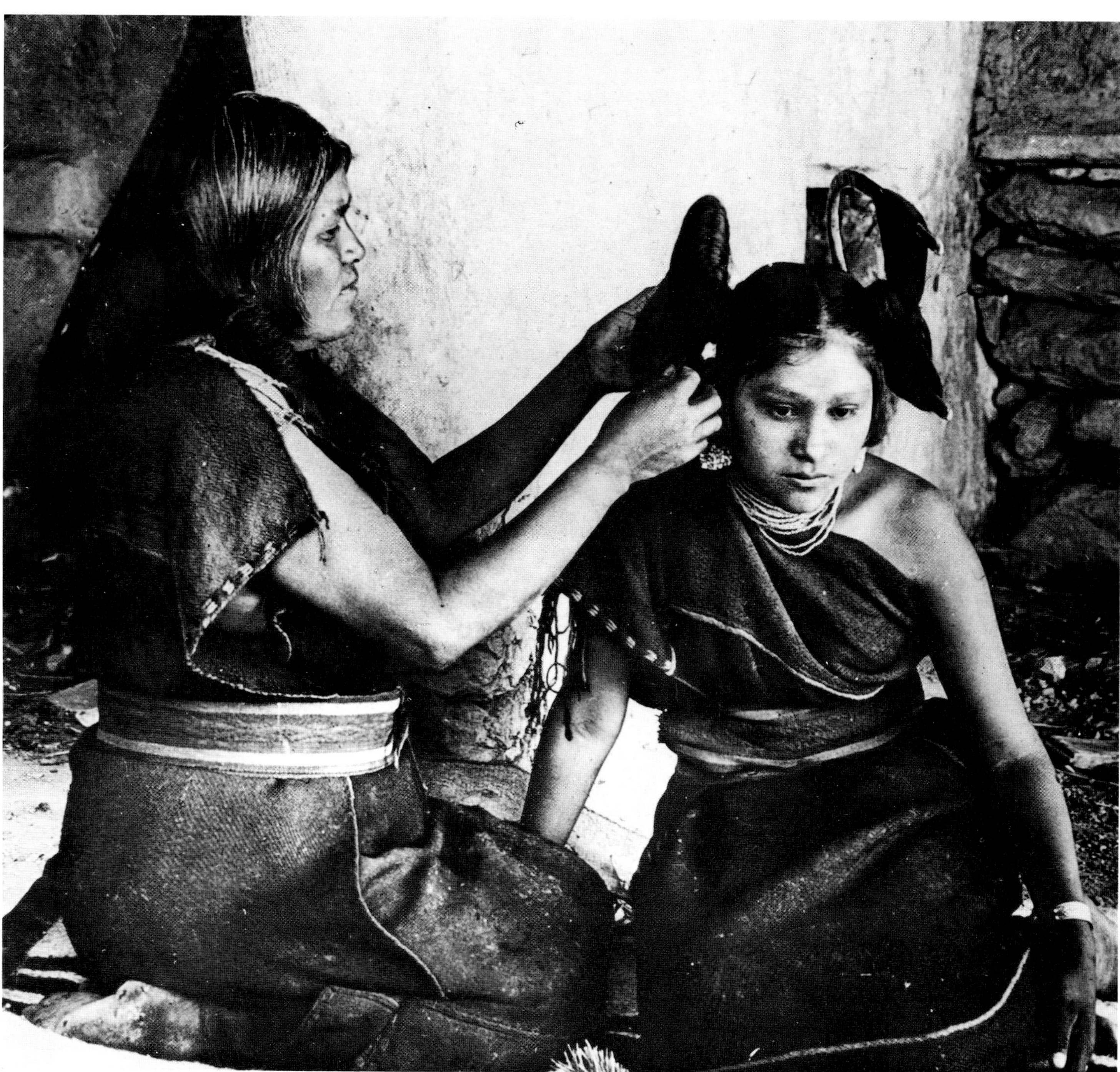

Above: A Hopi woman in the early 1900s is shown dressing the hair of an unmarried girl. After a four-day ceremony of grinding corn in a dark room, a young girl proved that she was skilled at household chores. The ritual concluded with an older woman preparing the elaborate squash-blossom hairstyle that was the sign of her marriageable status. The process required great skill and could take over an hour to finish. The hair was parted into two sections, and each section was wrapped around a U-shaped bow in a complex bun arrangement. After marriage the young woman braided her hair.

Indian Tribes of the Southwest

- **Apache**
  - **Chiricahua**
  - **Jicarilla**
  - **Lipan**
  - **Mescalero**
  - **Western**
- **Cahuilla**
- **Chemehuevi**
- **Cochimi**
- **Cupeno**
- **Halchidhoma**
- **Havasupai**
- **Hopi**
- **Maricopa**
- **Mojave**
- **Navajo**
- **Papago**
- **Pima**
- **Quechan**
- **Tonto**
- **Waiguri**
- **Walapai**
- **White Mountain**
- **Yaqui**
- **Yavapai**
- **Yuma**
- **Pueblos**
  - **Acoma**
  - **Cochiti**
  - **Galisteo**
  - **Isleta**
  - **Laguna**
  - **Jemez**
  - **Nambe**
  - **Pecos**
  - **Picuris**
  - **Pojoaque**
  - **San Felipe**
  - **San Ildefonso**
  - **San Juan**
  - **Sandia**
  - **Santa Ana**
  - **Santa Clara**
  - **Santo Domingo**
  - **Taos**
  - **Tesuque**
  - **Zia**
  - **Zuñi**

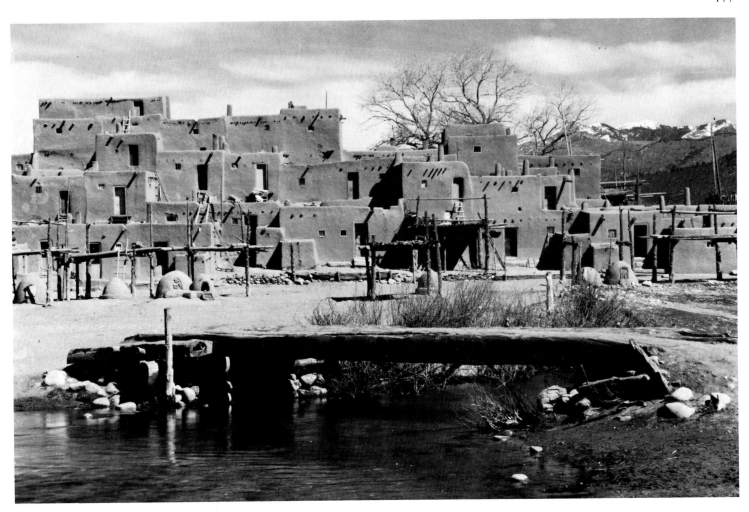

They were impersonated in costume by the men at the rituals and are also represented today by the popular and valuable Hopi Kachina dolls.

The white man first stumbled into the land of the Pueblos in the person of Cabeza de Vaca, a Spanish sea captain marooned on the Texas coast who led his men on a thousand-mile trek across the Southwest in search of a Spanish outpost. When they finally found their way to civilization they were filled with wild tales of seven cities of gold which were probably nothing more than the late afternoon sun shimmering on the walls of a distant adobe pueblo. A dozen years later Vasquez de Coronado led a mounted expedition up into the northern Rio Grande country, where, near the present city of Albuquerque, there was a concentration of Pueblos. Coronado pillaged the cities, finding no gold as expected, just corn and squash. The missionaries who went along to convert the savages not butchered by the soldiers set up missions alongside new Spanish cities. In 1680, however, the Indians revolted and destroyed the Spanish post at Santa Fe. Twelve years later the Spanish came back to Zuñi country, this time to stay, but they were not nearly so lucky in subduing the Hopis.

Though they inhabited the same region and had the same system of matrilineal descent, the Navajos had little else in common with the Pueblo people. When they arrived from the far north in the 1400s they were simply nomads. Their name in fact means gleaners in a Pueblo dialect. They were simple people but they learned quickly from the natives of the region. Their houses, called hogans, were simpler than the pueblos, but they adopted agriculture and eventually took to herding flocks of horses and sheep that they stole from the Spanish. The Navajo adulthood initiation was important in the overall cycle of tribal festivities,

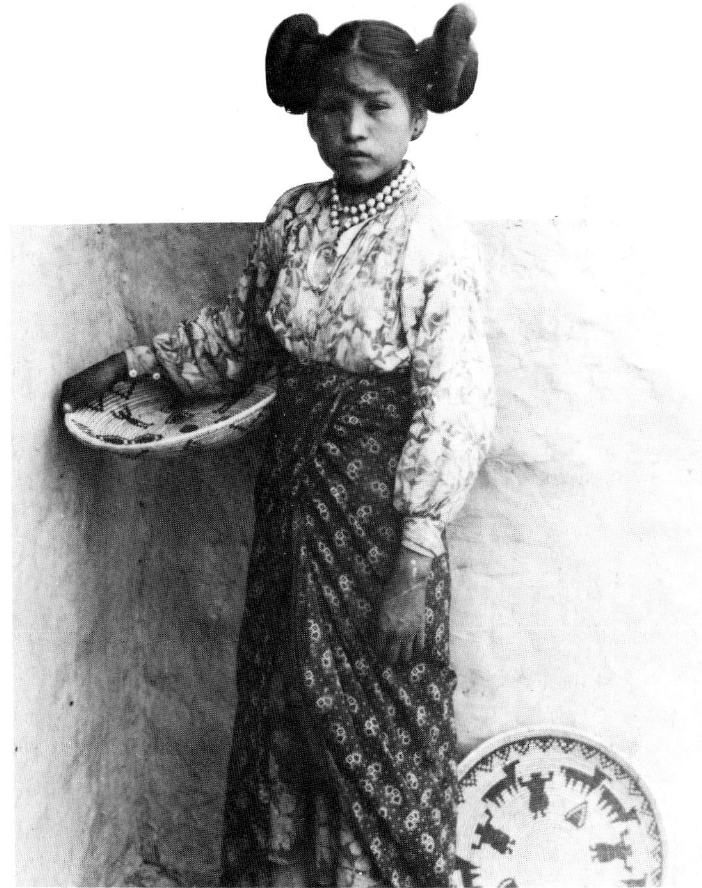

Top: The Rio Pueblo in the foreground divides the two high terraced communal dwellings that make up Taos Pueblo. Outside, at the front of the apartments, are the domed adobe ovens.

Above: An unmarried Oraibi girl from western Arizona displays her fine basketwork.

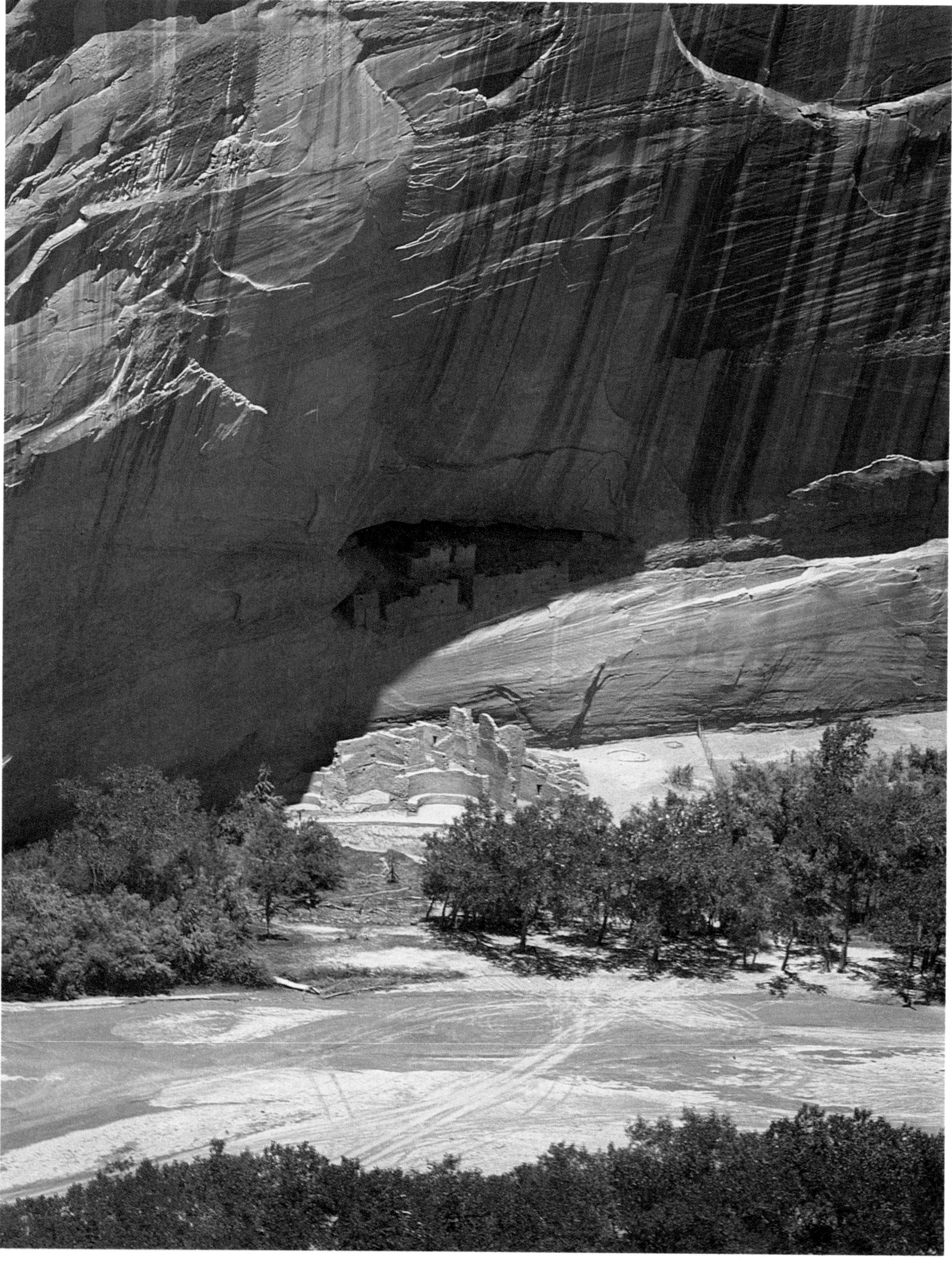

Above: The ruins of an Anasazi sandstone cliff dwelling, the White House, in Canyon de Chelly, Arizona are the remains of a complex ancient society. Many hundreds of Indians lived in this vast apartment complex and they became prosperous from farming the surrounding land. Many of their crafts have been preserved and have provided valuable evidence and insight into the level of that advanced culture. This ancient pueblo was discovered by whites by accident in the nineteenth century, and since then the area has been a paradise for archeologists.

Above: A contemporary Navajo hogan on the floor of Canyon de Chelly. Unlike the Pueblos, the Navajos lived in small isolated groups rather than in large organized villages. Their homes were compact earth-covered wooden lodges, circular in shape and with domed roofs. Navajos continue to live in traditionally built homes, but only the roof is covered with dirt. The doorway always faces east in honor of the sun. The Navajo were more organized as a tribe than their Apache cousins. They farmed as well as hunted, raised sheep and harvested their peach trees.

but not nearly as elaborate as the Hopi Kachina ceremonies. The onset of puberty in girls was treated with a good deal less of the arms-length approach seen among many other tribes in North America. After the elaborate coming-of-age rites, marriage among the tribes of the Southwest was anticlimactic. In fact, among the Navajos, the nuptial pact could be sealed by the man's bringing horses to give to the family of his intended.

Unlike the pueblo dwellers, the Navajo had little contact with the Spanish other than stealing a horse now and then. After the Mexican War in 1846, the Americans arrived in larger numbers than the Hispanics and replaced them in the Southwest. The mischief perpetrated by the Navajos and the Navajo retaliation for mischief perpetrated by whites raised the hackles of the US government and the Army was sent out to keep order. By 1862, with the Civil War raging in the East and the Army called away to fight other whites, the Navajos got the upper hand and were on the threshold of driving the white presence out of the Southwest. The government looked to legendary frontiersman Christopher "Kit" Carson for assistance. Carson was asked to put together an army of other frontiersmen who would be, like him, knowledgeable of the foe and the lay of the land. Their objective would be to drive the Navajo off their lands to a reservation at Bosque Redondo in New Mexico. Like the Vietcong of Southeast Asia a century later, the enemy was hard to find, impossible to force into a pitched battle, and he struck only when it suited *him.* The Navajo were also farmers, however, and needed their farms for subsistence. Carson therefore set about destroying whatever of their crops he could find, trampling their fields and stealing their sheep. In early 1864 the last of the

Above: This half-breed Indian woman from Wilcox, Arizona was a colorful character, half Irish and half Apache. She was photographed sometime before 1884.

Below: Geronimo (third from right, front), a Chiricahua Apache, resigned his peaceful ways after Mexicans killed his family. For two decades he led raids on the US Army but finally surrendered to the troops in 1886.

undefeated Navajo were cornered in Canyon de Chelly where they ultimately surrendered to Carson. By the end of the year the Navajo had been delivered to Bosque Redondo, where they tried to grow their own food. The land proved unsuitable for cultivation and they fell to living off government rations. Within four years it became obvious that the cost to the government of feeding this vast tribe was ridiculously high and a new reservation, the largest in the country, was granted to them in their old country, in northeastern Arizona.

The other major Athabaskan tribe to come to the Southwest retained the hunting and foraging lifestyle of its ancestors. The Apaches comprised a series of subtribes spread across the entire southwestern desert, from Arizona to Texas and south into Mexico. They had no organized civic structure, and like the Athabaskans of the far north, their leadership came not from a carefully designated chief but from the leader of an individual band who exhibited outstanding leadership traits. The first of these leaders to come to prominence among whites was a man called Cochise.

Relations had been generally good between the Apaches and the whites. Indeed, an 1852 treaty had a provision for mutual friendship forever. In 1861, however, things began to unravel. A part-white boy had been kidnapped. Cochise offered to help get him back, but was himself taken hostage. He escaped and guerrilla warfare broke out. Matters weren't helped when the following year his father-in-law, the highly regarded Mangus Colorado, was captured, murdered and mutilated by California volunteers while under a truce flag. The Apache guerrillas under Cochise eluded the Army and successfully kept it on the defensive

Above: Apache brothers Nalta and San Carlos, pictured in the 1880s, belonged to a warlike and loosely organized tribe. The Apaches were ruthless and ferocious warriors who were feared by all.

Below: Surrounded by pumpkin patches, a simple single-family Zuñi adobe blends perfectly with the western desert. Western Pueblo homes were built of stone and covered with clay.

Below: Sunset falls on a Navajo settlement about two hours north of the Navajo Nation capital at Window Rock in Arizona.

Left: A Navajo sheepherder tends his flock in Monument Valley. The Spanish introduced domesticated sheep to North America and the Navajos acquired

their herds by raiding Spanish holdings. Usually women owned the herds, but the men assumed the role of herder.

Right: A roadside souvenir stand south of the Navajo Reservation is a typical sight along Interstate 40, the old US Route 66.

Above: Masked "Mudheads" prepare to dance at the Zuñi Pueblo in New Mexico in 1879, while spectators line the upper walls. All Zuñi male youths were initiated into the Kachina Societies and during dances they wore masks to impersonate the spirits. Mudheads were clowns, the most well-known Kachinas, whose role was to entertain the audience. Among the Zuñi, culprits of incest were covered in mud as chastisement.

Left: Pima Indian Pfc Ira H Hayes at age 19 gets ready to jump during a training session at Marine Corps Paratroop School in 1943. He became famous as one of the four Marines who raised the American flag on Iwo Jima. Thousands of Indians served in the forces in World War II and many found it difficult to return to the poverty on the reservation. Ira Hayes became an alcoholic. Others became active in Indian affairs.

Above right: Tigua school children enjoy a break from the classroom.

Right: Cottage industries are the mainstay of economic life on the Navajo Reservation in northwestern New Mexico. Outside the hogan, several Navajo women contribute to the process of making the kind of rug they have become famous for. They card the wool with modern equipment, but spin the yarn on the old-style wooden spindle, twisting the wool into the required thickness. The Pueblos taught the Navajos the art of weaving; the novices learned quickly and turned out high-quality, intricately designed blankets and rugs.

Far right: An 1880 Navajo silversmith displays his work and his tools. The Navajos learned their trade from the Mexicans and created works of great beauty with primitive tools. Early jewelry was made from American or Mexican silver currency until sheets of the metal became available. The conchas shown here were used as hairpieces and also as belts.

for more than a decade. In 1872 General Oliver Otis Howard was finally able to meet with Cochise and negotiate a settlement. Under terms of the unique settlement Howard agreed that Cochise could have his own land as the Apache reservation and Cochise agreed that the Apaches would conclude their guerrilla warfare against the Americans. Two years later Cochise was dead of natural causes, and while most of the Apaches abided by the agreement, another Apache leader, one of Cochise's former lieutenants, decided to continue the war on his own. His name was Goyanthlay (one who yawns) but he is best known by the name given

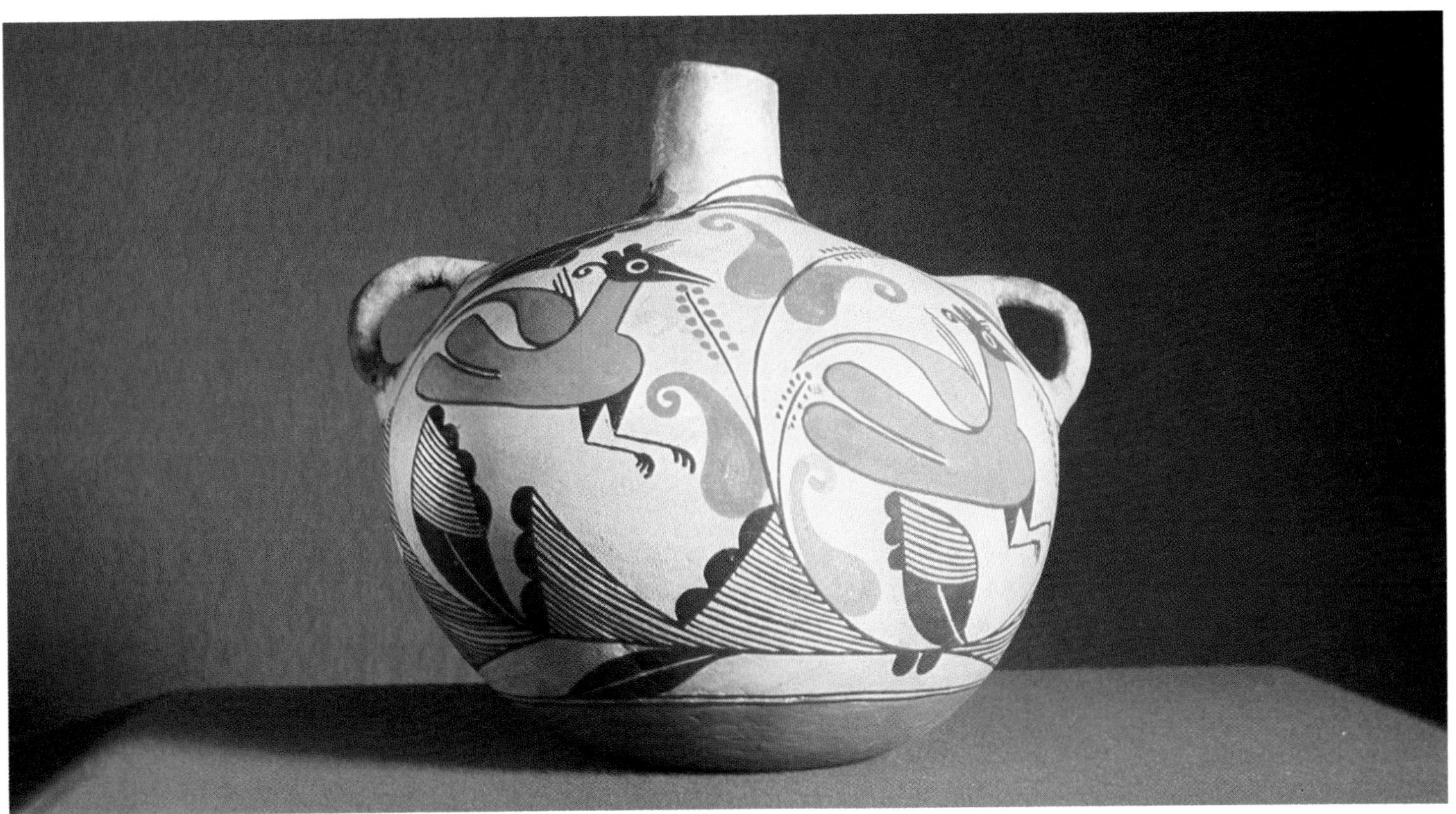

him by the Mexicans, Geronimo. He continued his raids against whites for five years until he was finally arrested and put on the San Carlos Reservation in 1877. He lasted there for three years before he broke out for another half-decade spree of looting and harassing the whites. He was finally captured in 1886 by General Nelson "Bearcoat" Miles and imprisoned, along with many of his followers, in Florida and later Alabama, where many of them died in the muggy humid air to which they were not accustomed. In 1894 Geronimo was transferred to Fort Sill, Oklahoma, where he was reduced to selling postcard photos of himself in his former glory. In his later years he became somewhat of a celebrity, or perhaps a curiosity, a novelty of a romantic bygone era. He was given an automobile to be driven around in, and in 1905 he was invited to Washington to ride in the inaugural parade of President Theodore Roosevelt. He never returned to the Southwest, however, and in 1909 he died at Fort Sill.

Although much of Indian culture has been destroyed or lost throughout North America, it still is prominent in the Southwest today. The pueblos are still thriving towns, the oldest continuously inhabited towns in North America. Pickup trucks and electricity have come, but otherwise life is surprisingly similar to what it must have been like centuries ago. In New Mexico the city of Taos, which has grown up near the Taos Pueblo, was reported by Citicorp/Diners Club in 1984 to be one of the four largest art markets in dollar volume in the world, surpassed only by Paris, New York and its neighbor Santa Fe. Much of the art being marketed features traditional Indian motifs and is executed by Indian artists. Across the border in Arizona the adjoining present-day Navajo and Hopi reservations take up an area the size of Connecticut and Rhode Island combined and are administered by the US government as a separate, fifty-first state. On the vast Navajo reservation the familiar highway patrol cars with the gum-ball lights on top bear the insignia, not of the Arizona State Patrol, but of the Navajo Nation.

Left and below: These Kachina dolls are likenesses of two Hopi spirits. The dolls are carved from cottonwood, painted and decorated with feathers or shells before the ceremony and presented to the children for study.

Above: The delicate and durable pottery of the Acomas is probably the finest produced by the Pueblos. Orange, red and black designs on a creamy white background are characteristic.

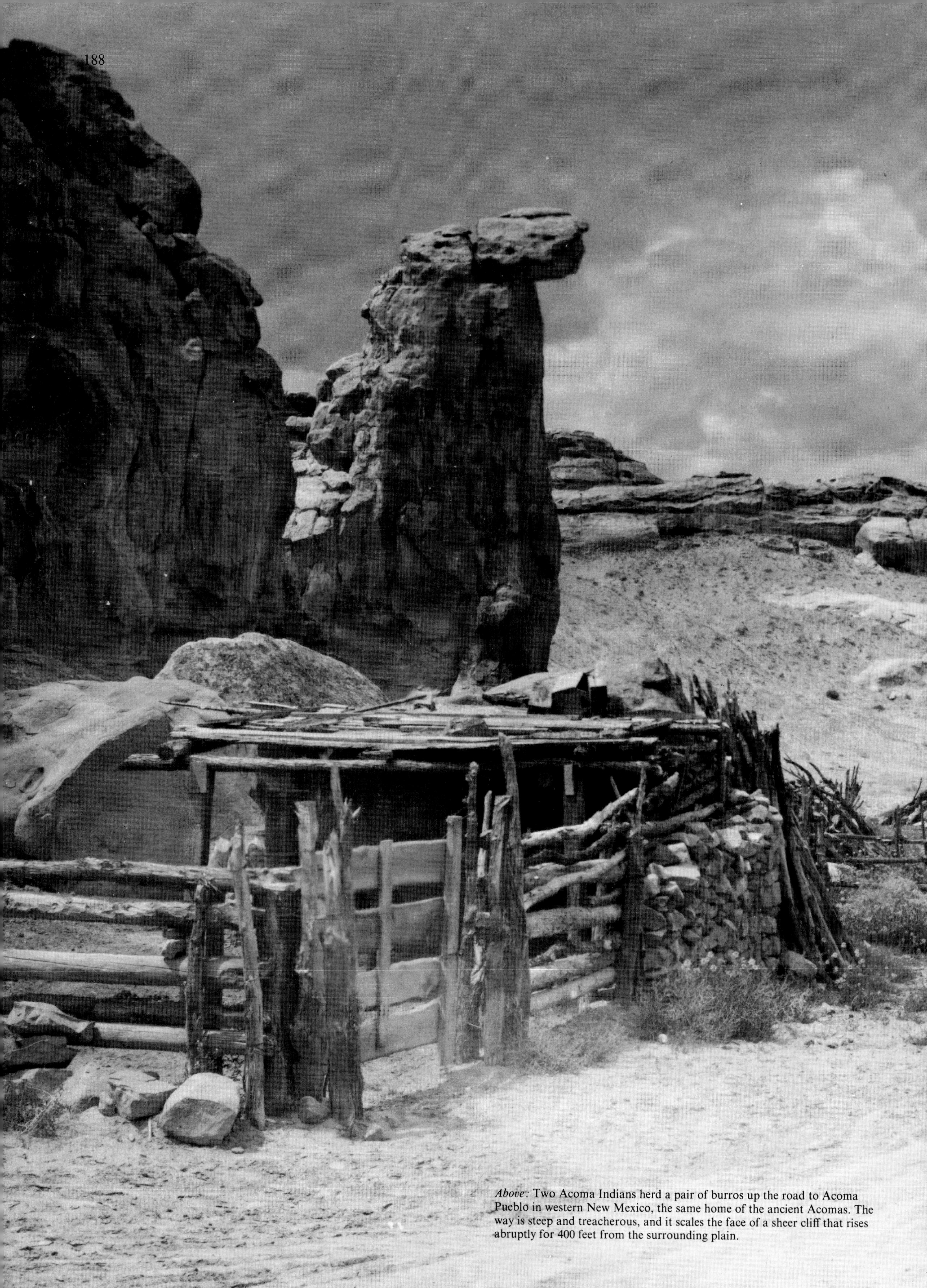

Above: Two Acoma Indians herd a pair of burros up the road to Acoma Pueblo in western New Mexico, the same home of the ancient Acomas. The way is steep and treacherous, and it scales the face of a sheer cliff that rises abruptly for 400 feet from the surrounding plain.

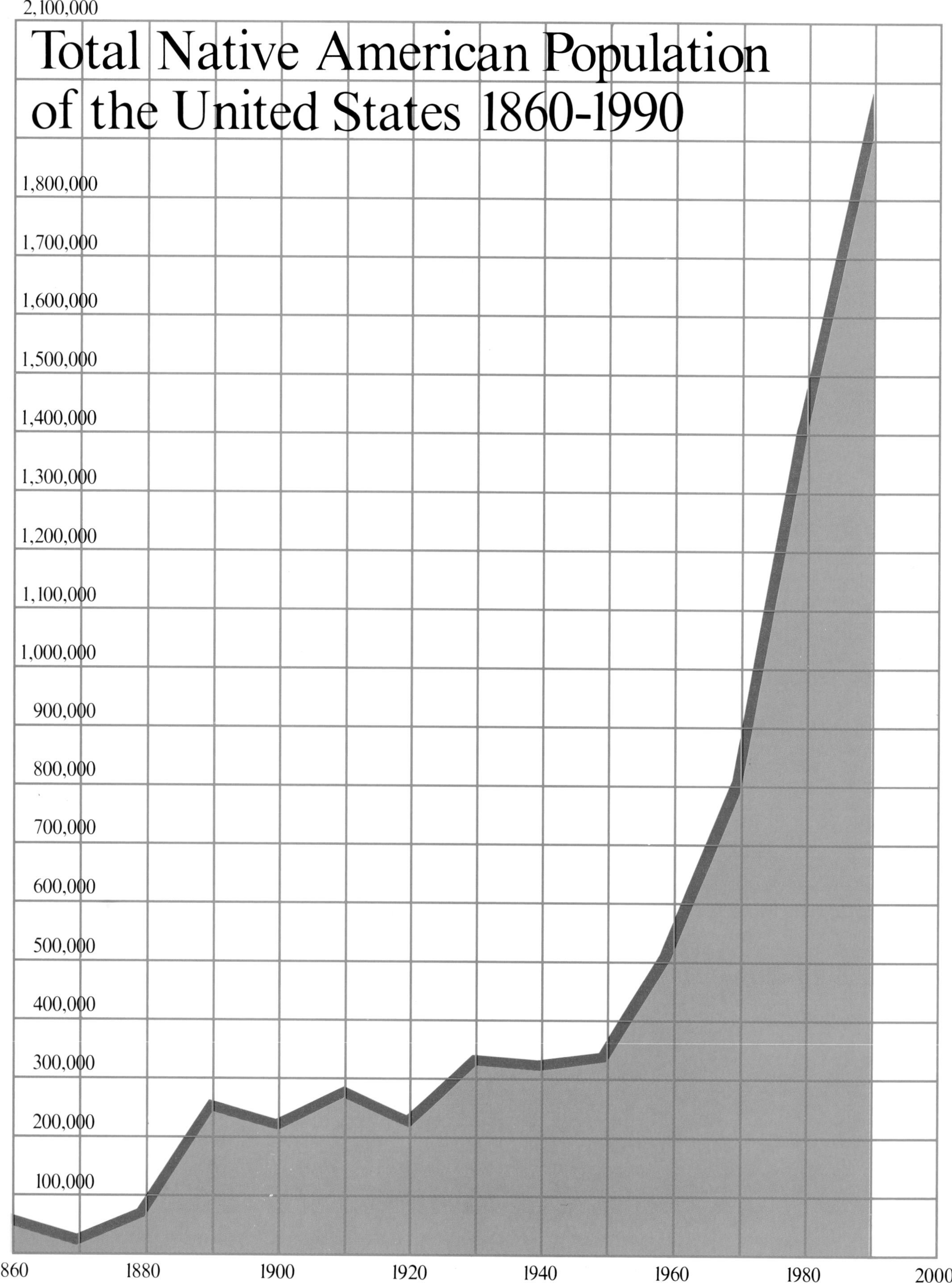

Note: The 1860 US census was the first in which the Native American population was counted as a separate group. Population estimates for the years prior to 1860 vary widely but are generally accepted to have been higher than the 1860 level. The Native American population probably averaged, for the preceding century, somewhere between the 1880 and 1890 levels.

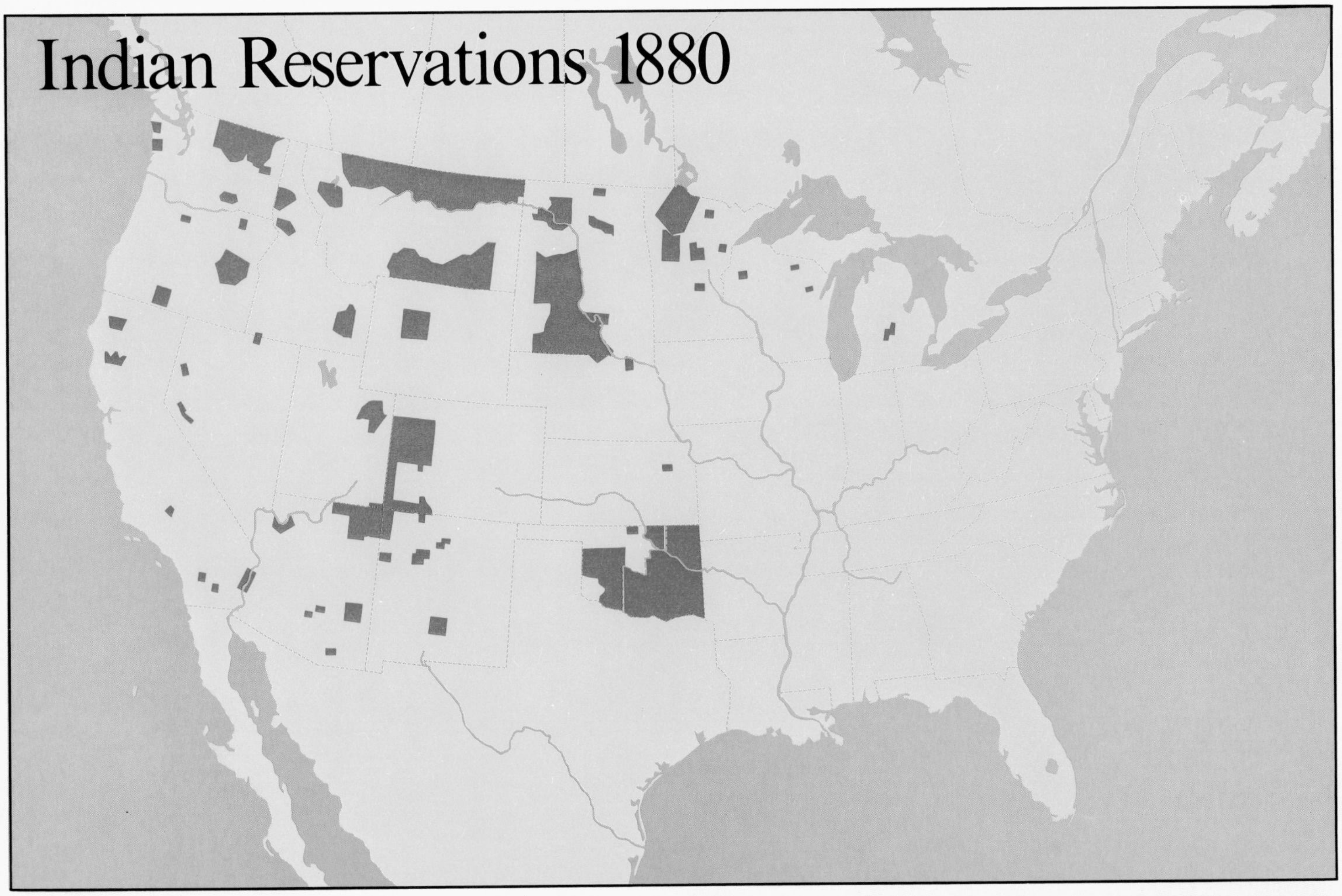

Indian Reservations 1880

Indian Reservations 1990

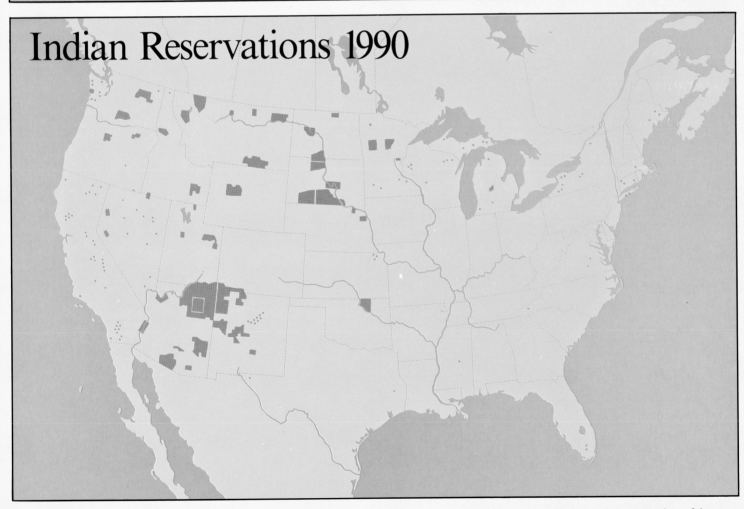

Above: These maps show the locations of Indian reservations as they existed at the time of the end of the Indian wars and as they exist today. In 1880 there were fewer and larger reservations, with the eastern half of the present state of Oklahoma designated Indian Territory. Today the huge reservations of the northern Plains are much smaller and the Navajo Reservation in Arizona (which completely surrounds the Hopi Reservation) is the largest.

Above: Paliwahtiwa was the governor of the Zuñi in the late 1880s. Most Pueblo Indian villages are organized into two political systems—one based on the system adopted from the Spanish and one based on the traditional Indian religious societies.